Lt. Robert O. Johnson

I'm Coming Home

Robert Orson Johnson

Trafford
PUBLISHING™

Printed in Victoria, BC, Canada.

ISBN: 978-1-4251-6856-8 (sc)

*Our mission is to efficiently provide the world's finest, most comprehensive
book publishing service, enabling every author to experience success.
To find out how to publish your book, your way, and have it available
worldwide, visit us online at www.trafford.com*

Trafford rev. 03/29/2010

 www.trafford.com

North America & international
toll-free: 1 888 232 4444 (USA & Canada)
phone: 250 383 6864 ◆ fax: 812 355 4082

Acknowledgements

My deepest appreciation to my brother, Norman Johnson, who contributed to the first page of my book, to my daughter, Suzanne Kelley, without whose dedication in typing and proof reading, this book would not have been possible, and I wish to thank Julie Lofurno and Steve and Joanna Young for their contribution. Thank you.

Dedication

This book is dedicated to my father and mother, Leslie and Eleanor Johnson, who never gave up hope that "I was coming home."

VNA787 45 GOVT=WUX WASHINGTON DC 18 734P

LESLIE S JOHNSON=   BA4 JUL 18 PM 8 04

FRENCH ROAD PITTSFORD NY=

THE SECRETARY OF WAR DESIRES ME TO EXPRESS HIS DEEP REGRET
THAT YOUR SON SECOND LIEUTENANT ROBERT O JOHNSON HAS BEEN
REPORTED MISSING IN ACTION SINCE SEVEN JULY OVER GERMANY IF
FURTHER DETAILS OR OTHER INFORMATION ARE RECEIVED YOU WILL
BE PROMPTLY NOTIFIED=

ULIO THE ADJUTANT GENERAL.

The Inevitable Telegram

The Inevitable Telegram

It was sometime between 5:45 and 6:00 on a pleasant evening in June of 1944. We, Mom, Dad, and I (Norm), were all at the table in the kitchen having supper when I heard someone come up on the porch at the front door. That was the first clue that something terribly wrong was about to happen.

I answered the knock that was made by the man from the Pittsford Post Office, someone I had seen many times before and later learned his name was Johnnie Cahill. He seemed very ill at ease and his countenance was very serious. He stammered that he had a telegram for a Mr. Leslie S. Johnson and was he here. I nodded and held out my hand for that yellow envelope which I dreaded to give to Dad. I turned and with a heavy heart handed the envelope to Dad, who opened it, read it, blanched, handed it to Mom, and then put his head down on his arms and cried. Mother read it, clutched it to her and said, "He's alright. I know he is coming home. He told me so!" She left the table dry eyed and went into the living room to just sit on the couch and stare at nothing.

Mother didn't cry then or at all until we received the telegram that told that Bob was taken Prisoner of War. She held herself together like a rock until that time and then she fell apart. She still kept saying, "He told me he would come home. I know he is coming home!"

Bob was liberated on April 29, 1945, very thin and quiet.

The Johnson Family: Back Row – Gene, Bob and Norman
Front Row – Eleanor and Leslie Johnson

Memories of Life
Rochester, New York
1922-1927

On a lovely day, my brother Gene and I were playing in water running down the sides of the street and into the storm gutters at the curbs. We had a vegetable can open at one end with which we dipped into the dirty water. As we splashed about, my brother, Gene, threw a whole can full of water right through the open window of a passing car and all over the beautifully dressed lady passenger sitting inside! The driver stopped his car, jumped out and chased us all the way home. As we ran inside and scrambled under a bed we heard a fierce knocking at the door which our mother was about to answer. The angry driver proceeded to tell mother what we had just done to him and his lady with mother saying she was sorry and that we would be punished for our crime. The gentleman left and we climbed out from underneath the bed and received a well deserved scolding during which we were told we would be given to the junkman when he and his wagon came again. The thought of being given to the dirty, old junkman with his old horse and wagon half full of trash was a fate close to death for two small boys. We promised not to do that again. . .or at least, not get caught!

At the age of seven, my family moved to East Rochester to West Elm Street, the same street where my mother's parents lived. Their names were Catherine and Camille DeVogler. Some of my earliest and best memories were the result of my grandmother giving me milk and cookies so that I would stay and play the game of Parchesi with her. Sometimes I'd sit and sing for hours, or so it seemed to a young child.

Our family names were Leslie Stephen Johnson (my father), Eleanor Celeste DeVogler Johnson (my mother), Robert Orson Johnson (me, the oldest) Eugene Leslie Johnson, (the middle brother), and Norman Lee Johnson (the youngest brother). Dad rented a home from the Yhondos that was a two-story framed single family home. My father's mother was with us until her early death from bronchitis shortly after we moved to East Rochester. This property had a single-car garage set apart unto the rear of the house. In it, Dad kept some rabbits in cages along with the feed for them. The chore of feeding and watering the rabbits fell on my brother, Gene, and I. One night after his workday, Dad drove into the yard and walked into the house and questioned whether we had fed the rabbits and we said that we had. Dad immediately told us to go outside to the driveway by the garage. There, scattered all over the ground was the rabbit feed. It seemed that Norman had dumped all the feed. . .the moral of this story is not to lie to your parents, especially to the one with the broad leather belt!

French Road

On July 4, 1932 we moved from East Rochester to French Road in Pittsford, New York to a piece of property owned by the state alongside the old Erie Canal. It was an old two-story house on 7 acres with a barn, chicken coop and a two-car garage attached.

In the early years of World War II, the Odenbach Company started a ship building operation in the deserted section of the Barge Canal at French Road. They featured an all-welded design that could traverse the Barge Canal east to the Hudson River and then south down the Hudson River to the New York Harbor. Once in the New York Harbor, the ships were completed for trans-ocean duty. This developed into a very successful enterprise. The shipyard worked around the clock during World War II.

In the mid 1930's, Dad and I started breeding pedigree New Zealand red and white rabbits. In a few years, we had established quite a business and reputation with the Bunny Dale Rabbitry and its show stock of all pedigreed rabbits which we sold as show stock at a good price. We developed and served meat markets with freshly butchered rabbit meat every Friday and Saturday. The show stock we exhibited at various rabbit shows throughout New York State. We accumulated quite a collection of show ribbons, including a number of Best-in-Show awards.

Our home on French Road was surrounded by meadows and woodlands. There was a lot of nature in those fields, especially field mice and rats. One day, my Dad decided to smoke out the rats that had come to spend the winter in our barn because he didn't want our rabbits to be infected by the rats. He told me to plug up all the holes around the floor of the barn. Then Dad attached a hose to the exhaust of his car and placed the hose underneath the barn. He started the car and I stood in the center of the barn floor waiting to see the results. Suddenly, with a great explosion, rats blew out of every hole I had covered and started running around my feet in crazed confusion. I was frantic and darted for the barn door with rats swirling around my feet.

I ran to the house shaking with fright. I never missed supper, but I did that night because I was in bed with the covers over my head. Needless to say, I hate rats to this day.

Having 7 acres, Dad decided to farm several of them. To properly prepare the soil, Dad designed and built a tractor from an old car by shortening the frame, removing the cab and installing dual wheels on the back with iron cleats on the real wheels for traction. Then, by attaching a plough to the rear of our homemade tractor, one of us would hold the plough while the other would drive. It was amazing how it worked!

When I was a boy of 16, my father decided to obtain a Billy goat that he had seen at a farm auction. He dealt with the goat's owner and proceeded to swap about ten of our better rabbits for it. One Friday afternoon after work, he and his friend, Mr. Roggie, drove our 7 passenger Studebaker with its back seat removed and swapped the rabbits for the Billy goat. On the way home, they proceeded to stop at various bar rooms to refresh themselves as they were prone to do out of long established habits. The major difference this time is that they entered into each establishment with the Billy goat on a long chain.

Now to appreciate the situation, you should picture what this goat looked and smelled like. The goat was a mixture of red, yellow and shades of brown and black. He had large, curly horns with a single complete twist so that their points were forward. His favorite pastime was to urinate in his generous 6 inch beard and then shake his head so that his sprinkling would cover his entire body and the odor alone was intimidating. Add to the view, this animal was jumping and prancing at the end of a length of chain held back by my father and his friend, this caused quite a disturbance in the bar and they were readily invited to immediately leave the premises. This scene was repeated again and again coming from the west side of the city to the east side of the city straight to the Johnson home. Needless to say, the three Johnson boys were excited at the presence of this new and highly energetic animal. At Dad's instructions and with his help, we took the Billy goat to one of the large apple trees out in the orchard and added a length of rope to the chain so the goat could walk and pasture in 360 degrees unless the weather was bad and then he was brought inside the barn with the rabbits.

During the next several months, Gene and I had lots of fun riding Billy. We'd put a burlap sack over the goat's back and climbed on whereby Billy planted all four feet and refused to go in whatever direction. We only applied means of friendly persuasion with a long stick to goose him. Look out! Immediately, Billy shot forward with a rapid jump to the end of his 100 foot chain to an abrupt stop. The unwanted passenger was duly discharged over Billy's head onto the grassy orchard floor. Fortunately, Gene and I repeated the wild ride time and time again without any broken bones. However, we came away smelling like stinky Billy much to our mother's distress.

The Johnson's newspaper boy, Pete Connors, wanted very much to ride Billy. Gene and I finally said that Pete could ride and we instructed him to come onto the burlap saddle and to hold on. Pete rode to the end of the chain only to fall off as we did. When he returned home one evening, his mother sent him out to the back door, handed Pete a change of clothing and sent him to their garage to change. Pete was then told never to ride the Johnson goat again.

Gene and I realized that goat riding was fun but dangerous so we decided what we needed was a goat cart. We tore apart a grocery cart to obtain four wheels, used old railroad car siding boards from Dad's scrap lumber pile and built a platform with Billy upfront in a rope harness. We rode up and down the black top road in front of our house having the time of our lives, thanks to Billy.

Unfortunately, the incident that followed put an end to Billy's stay at the Johnson's house. One day, Billy broke off part of his chain and catching a view of me, he took up the chase round and round the house with me screaming for help as I ran. By the time Gene came out of the house, Billy had me pinned against the barn door with his horns pointed forward leaving just enough space for me to turn my body to one side. Gene managed to tie a rope around Billy's neck and then over the overhead beam inside the barn. A brief pull on the rope lifted Billy away to release me and then our goat was immediately retied to the tree in the orchard. That night when Dad got home from work, he was informed by our very upset Mother about the day's events. Truly, that goat had to go and was sold off at a nearby farm auction shortly thereafter.

The Franklin Square Gas Station

The Franklin Square Gas Station

The Franklin Square Gas Station and Parking Lot was built by the Odenbach Company on Franklin Square in Rochester, New York.

My father, being a long time employee of the Odenbach Company Stone Quarry, was offered the management position of the newly constructed gas station and parking lot. The gas station was located down the street from the Odenback Bakery. The manager of the bakery, a relative of the Odenbach's, lived enroute on our way to the gas station and was convenient to provide him transportation to and from work. One of the fringe benefits was the two large boxes of assorted baked goods that were given to us every Friday evening.

The employees of the gas station were furnished with sharp uniforms and our gas station prospered for the next ten years until a discount gasoline station opened across Franklin Square Park and subsequently, we were forced to sell the business. Six months later, we opened a Rotary Station on East Avenue adjacent to a branch railroad crossing.

World War II came along and Dad went to work as a plant foreman. A year later, we closed the gas station and I went to work for John Redman and was in charge of their main stone crusher.

Bob & Dad (Top)
J.H. Pesso, Crossing Guard (Bottom)

Ramblings
By J.H. Pesso

If you want to get some service
This is going to be a fact.
You go right out East Av-en-ue
Just over the railroad track.

Now don't get this wrong
As I'm making this quite clear.
Just look for the Rotary Station
And you'll have nothing more to fear.

Then you swing in Les' station
Try this just for fun.
Les charges out to meet you
As he's always on the run.

Les is a right guy
He don't go much for style.
But every time you see him
He always has a smile.

You may want some oil
Or you may want some gas.
You may want your tires checked
Which gets attention last.

If you ever get a car
And it has no pull at all,
Drive right down to Les' place
and get some Rota-zol.

If you have an oil burner
And you find it a big expense,
Try Les' Kerosene oil
For seven and one half cents.

Now Les has two helpers
Who's names are Gene and Bob.
Both are high school students
And are always on the job.

Gene cleans your windows
While Bob serves you gas.
Gene checks the oil
But Bob takes the cash.

Gene and Bob are brothers
They don't go in for boxin.
Their dad you heard so much about,
His full name's Leslie Johnson.

Gene weighs 180
Bobby 164
It won't be long now before Geney
Can put Bobby upon the floor.

Bobby is all for business
Geney is all for fun
But when it comes to service cars
Both boys are on the run.

Bobby has a Ford
a coupe to be exact
He goes any place at all
And always makes it back.

His Dad has got a Buick
He thinks it's pretty good,
But every time I look for him
His head's under the hood.

That Les's car is a lemon
Anyone can see.
But don't tell Les I said so

He may take a poke at me.

I don't know Mrs. Johnson
I mean not very well.
Judging the rest of the family
She certainly must be swell.

There is still another brother
That you sure would like to know.
When he smiles he has two dimples
And his hair is white as snow.

Raising rabbits is his hobby
Norman Johnson is his name.
He don't believe in Santa Claus,
But still he got a train.

Now if you'd like to meet them,
This is going to be a fact.
You go right out East Av-en-ue
Just over the railroad track.

When Jim Ransom came back to Pittsford after enlisting in the Marine Corp., I fell in love with his Marine dress uniform. I thought it was one of the most beautiful uniforms that I had ever seen and naturally made up my mind that I was also going to enlist in the Marine Corp.

I already registered for the draft because I was still too young to be called up for duty. Therefore, in order to enlist, I needed consent papers from my parents which they reluctantly gave me. I immediately went down to the local Marine Recruiting Office to enlist into the Marine Corp. After the usual physical, they told me that before they could swear me in I would have to have my tonsils removed.

I agreed and went to my doctor and made the necessary arrangements for the operation. I also decided to be circumcised at the same time. While lying in the hospital bed recovering from the operation, Allen Esker, a neighborhood friend of mine came in to visit me. Allen said that he understood that I was going to become a Marine. I said that was correct and I was signing up as soon as I was out of bed. Allen said, "Are you crazy? You're going to get yourself killed on one of those Pacific Islands. Why don't you join the Army Air Force with me for pilot training? Upon graduation, you get 2nd Lt. bars, wings, a beautiful uniform and a much higher salary then you would as a Marine." Allen persuaded me to become a pilot. Unfortunately, Allen washed out in flight training school but did become a tail gunner on a B-17 bomber. I went on and became a B-24 pilot after months of training.

Bob and his Mother

Lt. Robert O. Johnson, Pittsford, NY

Training Begins
Letters From The Heart Of A Cadet

(1)
Pvt. Robert O. Johnson
Co. E 1213 R.C.
Ft. Niagara, NY

Mr. L. S. Johnson
French Rd.
Pittsford, NY

Dear Folks,

     Just a line to let you know that I am well &
happy. Haven't had time to write a letter as yet.
Called for unexpected K.P. at 5:30 this morning.
Worked until 7:00 PM without stop except for
meals. Received more clothes yesterday than I have
at home. Please write to above address.

                               Bob

(2)
U.S Army
October 31, 1942

Dear Folks,

     It's raining here today, so for the first time
since arriving here, I have a few free minutes to

myself. Excuse me for a few moments—they just blew the whistle for chow.

Here I am again. We had hot dogs, beans, boiled potatoes, salad and onions for supper. The eats are swell here. Every meal is different and plentiful. We had chicken for dinner.

We left Rochester 6:27 Tuesday night on the NYC for Buffalo. I phoned Red at the plant and told him the time I was leaving. I thought perhaps you would see me off, but I am glad you didn't after seeing all the other parents standing around sobbing. We arrived in Buffalo about 7:45 then took a bus to Fort Niagara.

Upon arriving here they gave us coffee and sandwiches. Then they gave us a duffel bag with our bedding and also gave us a raincoat. We then went into the barracks (they are a long wooden building with approx. 45 beds in each) and made our beds and went to sleep. The next morning we got up at 6:00, washed and went to breakfast.

We then marched to a building and took a Mechanical test. Then they marched us to the other end of the Fort and gave us a lecture on bonds and life insurance. I bought a $10,000 policy. It will cost $6.50 a month until I become a flying cadet and then I will automatically get it free of charge. It was then dinnertime. After dinner we marched to another building and received two shots—one in each arm. The one in the right arm really makes it sore. In the same building we received 80 lbs. of clothing. Boy, you really get beautiful clothing and plenty of it. Then we had a personal interview and took another test. They then took us to supper.

When they issued our clothes to us, they were all stuffed into one duffel bag. They gave us 2 summer suits, 2 fatigue suits and two dress suits plus a heavy winter over-coat, 3 pair of light socks, 3 pair of heavy socks, 2 sweatshirts, 3 sets of light underwear, dress coat, 3 hats, 2 pair of heavy shoes, 2 sets of winter underwear, 3 ties, 3 white handkerchiefs, canvass putties, belt, gabardine windbreaker, and a rain coat. If I missed anything I am sorry. While all this stuff was packed in a duffel bag in any old way, what do you think happened? At 5:30 that next morning, somebody with a flashlight wakes me up and tells me to report in 5 minutes for K.P. duty—that is kitchen police.

It wouldn't be bad if you could turn some light on, but lights don't go on until 6:00. I didn't know what to do, so I woke up the fellow next to me and he kept lighting book matches until I found my fatigue clothes. I worked until 7:00 PM in the kitchen. We only feed about 1,200 men in our kitchen so you can imagine the amount of work.

I went to the theatre last night and, as I was coming out, I ran into Allen Esker. That was quite a surprise, for I never dreamed he was in camp. He told me he's been here for 12 days.

All air cadets are slow on being shipped out, for there is very little room for them as all air bases are overloaded now.

A person is crazy to bring anything, for the army furnishes everything. Comb, razor, blades, toothbrush. All you need to bring in shaving cream and toothpaste. What I need and wish you would send to me just the moment you receive this letter is my pocket flashlight. I need it. Send it quick, for you never know when you are going to be shipped out. There are a swell bunch of fellows here. I have about 10 pals. The food is good, beds are good, weather is nice, and I was never happier in my life.

Army life is great for a fellow, but it is all hard work, almost as bad as Redman's.

Yesterday I was on a truck detail. They took us about 10 miles outside of Camp and we filled 4 trucks with topsoil.

They use the topsoil here in camp for grading off the woods.

There is a prisoner here that pounds huge rocks with a sledge hammer all day long. The rock is so hard that it doesn't chip off but turns to powder just like baking flour. He does this every day. He only has 7 years to go. He is an example of what happens to you if you desert from the army. It just doesn't pay.

Love to all, Bob

My address is: Pvt. Robert O. Johnson, Co. E, 1213 R.C., U. S. Army, Fort Niagara, NY

P.S. Always be sure to put the O. in as it is important. There are lots of Robert Johnsons in the Army.

(3)
Service Club
Forth Niagara, New York
Nov. 1, 1942

Hello Folks,
      Pardon the two letters at once, but I wrote
the first letter last night and didn't put it in the mail.
This morning I was glad that I didn't, for this
morning we were told that we are going to be
shipped out, where I don't know. Allen Esker is
also being shipped out today. All of the fellows
being shipped today are Aviation Cadets.
      Because of this change, please do not send
my flashlight until you receive my new address.
      Who else do you suppose is here at Fort
Niagara? Bill Baar is here. He is in the same
company as I am. That is company E.
      Today is Sunday, so it is a day off. I am
writing this in the Service Club. It is a long
building all decorated up, with plenty of chairs and
tables for playing games, writing etc. There is a
radio, plenty of books, and also an ice cream
fountain.
      Thanks for forwarding those two letters to
me.

                       Love as ever, Bob

(4)
Pvt. Robert O. Johnson
U.S. Army

Leslie S. Johnson
French Rd.
Pittsford, New York

Arrived in New York City 7:30 this
morning. Swell day. We are going to be at
Mitchell Field for a while.

(5)
Fort Niagara, New York
November 4, 1942

Salutations,
We came on train from Fort Niagara to
Mitchell Field, Long Island. We left Niagara about
6 o'clock Sunday night and arrived in New York
City at 7 AM Monday morning. We hung around
Grand Central Station for about 1 hr. waiting for 10
Army trucks to take us to the Penn Sta. We ate
dinner there. We took a train from Penn Sta. to
Mitchell Field, Long Island.
Mitchell Field is right outside of Hempstead,
New York. The weather is fine here, but cold at
night. I have just come off a 24-hr. guard duty. We
patrol for 2 hrs. and sleep for 4 hrs. You patrol 8
hrs. out of 24. The rest of the time you sleep in
tents around the guardhouse. The tents are all right,
but half of them you couldn't build fires in them.

We froze in our tent. I couldn't stand after the first 4-hr. rest period and moved into another tent where they had a fire. After you carry a gun across your shoulder for a 2-hr. stretch, your arm gets numb. That's why this writing is so rotten.

The sky is full of planes at all times. You get so used to them that you don't stop to notice them half the time. There are all types, bombers light and heavy, and pursuit planes. There are a large number of P-47 Republic Thunderbolts. They are new, but considered the best of our pursuit ships.

We are not camped on Mitchell Field, but on a sub-post right outside of the field. It is called Camp Mills. The place is overcrowded. As I understand it, we will be here only for a short period. We will eventually be shipped to a classification center. The possibilities are Tennessee, Texas, and California.

All we do here is drill, K.P. and guard duty. After we have been here a week, we can get passes to leave the post. We can go to Mitchell Field, Hempstead, or New York City on these passes.

Tomorrow I am going to get 2 more shots in the arm. I'll have a sore arm for a day or so. I am in good health except for a slight cold I caught last night. I have bought some Vapor Rub. We can get all the medical attention we want if we need it.

Say hello to Norman and Gene. How are they? Tell Gene that if he likes hard work to get in the Army for you get plenty of it. Please excuse the writing.

Your loving son, Bob

P.S. Please send my pocket flashlight

(6)
USO, United Service Organization
Nov. 5, 1942

Dear Folks,
        I am writing this in the U.S.O. in
Hempstead. It is a beautiful building for soldiers. I
bought myself a Garrison hat tonight like the
officers wear.
        My cold is getting better. I worked on a
detail today making an outdoor basketball court.
        This paper is free so I'll write on one side
only.
        It was a nice day today, but cold in the
morning. I put on my winter underwear. It is a
sweatshirt and pants that are just the same as long
underwear.
        This is my first night outside of the post. I
stopped at a tailor's and had the air corps wings
sewed on coat and shirt.
        I am dong an awful job of writing this letter
but it is the pen's fault. It belongs to the U.S.O.

There is news of a big shipment leaving here pretty
soon. Perhaps I'll be in it, I hope so. Allen Esker is
here with us if I haven't told you before.

                Love as ever, your son, Bob

(7)
Pvt. Robert O. Johnson
Army Air Base Sub Post #2
Mitchell Field New York

Norman L. Johnson
French Road
Pittsford, New York

Hello Fatty, How's school? I'm surprised at you.
I've been in the Army a week and a half and you
haven't written.

 (8)
Pvt. Robert O. Johnson
Army Air Base Sub Post #2
Mitchell Field, New York

Eugene L. Johnson
French Road
Pittsford, New York

Hi Kid, how is your job? This camp here is terrible.
You work on Sundays here. Why not drop me a
line?

(9)
Pvt. Robert O. Johnson
Army Air Base Sub Post #2
Mitchell Field, New York

Mr. & Mrs. Leslie S. Johnson
French Road
Pittsford, New York

I have to go on guard duty at 4:00 PM. Have news
that we'll be shipped out about Nov. 18. I hope so.

(10)
U.S. Army
Nov. 9, 1942

Dear Folks,
        Received your letter this afternoon and was
very happy to do so.
        I just this moment came off a 24 hr. guard
duty. However this time I slept all night long, for I
was what they call here a "supernumerary". That
means a substitute in case any of the other guards
are taken ill or has visitors, etc.
        I went to the doctor yesterday morning for
my cold. He examined me thoroughly. He gave me
some cough medicine and an order for a quilt for
my bed. He said my lungs were clear. My cold has
greatly improved today. That comforter for my bed
will be a great help for I have been cold in bed
nights.
        I am glad to hear that Gene's job turned out
so well. Tell him to stick to it, for $50 a week is
much better than $50 a month.

My flashlight hasn't arrived yet, but I will certainly be glad to receive it.

I am sorry to hear that Dad and Gene tried so hard to see me off at the station and missed me, but they shouldn't feel so bad about it for I was about the only happy fellow to board that train. The rest of the fellows had their parents and relatives there sobbing all over the place, consequently making the boys rather sad about departing.

Incidentally, about 300 more men arrived here today. This is a good sign that we will be shipped from here in a week or so.

I am beginning to find it hard to write, for the same thing happens here day after day. Rarely anything of excitement ever happens. However, I have been here a week today and am now able to get passes to leave the Camp at night and go to town.

There is a big U.S.O. in Hempstead. They give dancing lessons there. If I am here long enough I am going to attend a few classes.

No! I didn't see Francis at Fort Niagara. Do you have his address?

Will write again tomorrow.

Love, Bob

(11)
Pvt. Robert Johnson
Army Air Base
Mitchell Field
Sub-Post #2 New York

Mrs. Leslie S. Johnson
French Rd.
Pittsford, New York

      Leaving this afternoon for what we believe will be San Antonio, Texas. I use the word private because that is what we are until we make the grade. Using words Air Cadet is being too optimistic.

                                    Bob

(12)
L.S. Johnson
French Rd.
Pittsford, New York

Dear Folks,
      This card is being tossed out the window of our train to be mailed by whomever catches it. Going thru Missouri Nov. 18, 10:45 AM. Been on train since Mon. 10 o'clock PM.

                                      Bob

(13)
U.S. Army
Nov. 16, 1942

Hello Folks,
      A great many things have happened since I last wrote you.
      First, my cold is practically gone except for a productive cough.
      Today I received a partial pay. They gave me $15.00. This is because they are shipping us out tomorrow or the next day. This afternoon we will receive our ration money. This is money we use to buy our meals on the way to our classification center. We are almost sure that we are going to San Antonio, Texas, but not positive.
      Last Tuesday I went to New York City with a friend of mine. His name is Joe Pasner. He is 6 foot 2 inches. He is a Jewish kid of 18 and a very swell fellow. We went to the Stage Door Canteen. This is a recreation center for service men only. Everything there is free. They give you sandwiches, coffee, milk, fruit, candy. There are also all kinds of girls to talk and dance with. They are all radio or stage girls.
      One girl taught me three different dance steps and I was dancing all evening having a swell time. I did very well according to the girls. They couldn't believe that I had never danced before.
      The girl that taught me how to dance is the girl that takes the part of Irene on the radio program of "Just Plain Bill".
      Wednesday there was a very bad automobile accident just about a mile from camp. A taxi with 8 soldiers in it went through a stop street and another

car ploughed right into it. One soldier from our camp was killed outright. His name was Thomas Lee. Another fellow from our camp was injured and he also died yesterday. Two other soldiers were also killed in this accident, but they were from Mitchell Field.

I received a letter from Bill Stark and also one from Bill Horrod this week. Bill Stark is getting his basic training and, according to him, they are just about killing him. They have 275 men in his company. There are 75 of this number in the hospital with broken bones of every description.

Bill is going t to try to get a transfer to another Co. He is a truck driver.

Bill Horrod said in his letter, "Write home every day even if it's only a line, they sure like to hear from you, and you want mail also!"

He was certainly right about that for mail is certainly appreciated. It takes the monotony off things. You never realize what a letter means until you get into the service. He also gave me some other good advice.

I received Gene's letter, which was very interesting. I will answer his letter later on for I am in a hurry as you can tell by the mistakes in this letter.

By the way, Horrod would appreciate a letter from Dad. He has mentioned this to me several times.

Your loving son, Bob

(14)
Nov. 22, 1942

Hello Folks,
        Left New York Tuesday night 10:15 PM.
Arrived at Kelly Field, San Antonio, Texas Friday 3
PM.
        Briefly, our trip took us from New York
across Jersey to Philadelphia, from Philadelphia to
Pittsburgh, then across the tip of West Virginia to
Columbus, Ohio. We left Columbus on to
Indianapolis and then to St. Louis, Missouri. At St.
Louis, we changed from day coaches to Pullmans.
From New York to St. Louis, we traveled on the
Pennsylvania railroad. At St. Louis, we changed
over to the Missouri Pacific. This was 2:00
Thursday morning.
        The trip through the states of Missouri and
Arkansas was the worst part of the trip. The
conditions of those two states, at least through the
parts we traveled, are pitiful. The landscape is a
mess of scrub trees, vines, and wet lowlands. The
people live in a real state of poverty. They live in
unpainted shacks of one or two rooms that are built
of scrap lumber or logs. They all seem to have a
dozen kids in those conditions. Their only visible
means of support were their fields of cotton and
corn. For the first time in my life I saw cotton on
the bush ready for picking. The climate in those
states at this time of the year is warm and sticky.
We stopped at Poplar Bluff, Missouri for about 15
minutes Thursday afternoon. We got off the train
for the first time since leaving New York.
        From Poplar Bluff we went on down to
Little Rock, Arkansas. From there on to Texas, the
scenery improved gradually. The part of Texas we

came through was also wild and poor. The scenery is very pretty in spots, but the shacks the people live in along the railroad mar this. However, the houses away from the railroad are small, but nice. There is cactus all over of the same type as the big one at home. The cities here are beautiful. They are very progressive. Their buildings all seem new and very modernistic.

Kelly Field is located about 20 miles south of San Antonio, Texas. This is a brand new field, but enormous. We are living in brand new barracks that are two stories high. They are shingled gray with cream trimmings. Each barracks has its own showers, toilets and drinking fountains. In the other camps there were in separate buildings and were used by 3 or 4 other barracks beside your own.

We have individual lockers for our clothing and other articles. The food is wonderful. We have nothing but the best and all we want of it.

For dinner today we had chicken, mashed potatoes, gravy with noodles, cabbage and egg salad, peas, fruit salad with nuts, ice cream, angel food cake with strawberry frosting, orangeade, and coffee. We have milk for breakfast and supper. It is more like cream. The caps on the bottles say for coffee and cereal.

I received my appointment as Aviation Cadet on the day we were shipped from New York. I have now the right to put the words aviation cadet before my name instead of private. That means I am now making $75 a month and my $10,000 insurance policy is free.

As aviation cadets we are neither enlisted men nor officers. We are nothing. We are called Mister So-and-So. We don't just walk around a corner, but cut all corners square with a pivot. We eat with the right hand on the table only. The left hand is on our laps. We don't talk needlessly or laugh at the table. We have to be polite at all times and to everyone. We can't spit outside around the barracks. Our personal appearance has to be perfect at all times. There are many other things, but I can't just think of them all.

After and if we are classified as pilots, etc. we receive our cadet caps, accessories, and other clothing. They look as nearly like officers as possible.

Most fellows pass the classification. Most fellows wash out later on in Pre-flight and in Primary and Basic flight. If you wash out here, it is for physical reasons only. If you wash out later on, it is because you are not learning fast enough to suit them or else you just are not suited for the air.

If you wash out, you are given ground duty in the air corps.

I am neither worried about passing nor really care too much. If it is intended for me to be a good pilot I will. If it is otherwise, that is the way it was meant to be.

I wish you would all write to me for it is pleasant to receive mail. On the other hand, I wish you all would allow me to answer your letters as a whole to the family in a single letter like this. If I write 4 different letters home, it is difficult to say something different to each one.

I could use my camera down here. I wish you could send that to me along with my Bible. If you send them to me by first class mail they would get here much faster. It is a long way down here.

I have a 50-mm machine gun shell for Norman that I will send to him just as soon as I get a chance. I was glad to get that letter from both

Gene and Norman. Norman doesn't have to worry
about men and the girls, for there just aren't any
around here.

Your son, Bob

P.S. Has dad got back from his hunting trip? If so,
how did he make out?

(14A)
U.S. Army
11/26/42

Hello Folks,

Happy Thanksgiving! I certainly missed not
being home today, but they treated us swell here in
an effort to make it up to us. On top of having a
beautiful turkey dinner for us, they gave each Cadet
a ½ lb. box of chocolate creams, a package of
cigarettes and a cigar. I gave the cigar and
cigarettes away and ate the candy.

In the morning before dinner, I took the
army "64" physical examination. I passed
everything O.K. except for my blood pressure,
which was a little high. My pulse was perfectly
normal this time. I am not worried about this,
however, for it wasn't very much too high.

If my blood pressure turns out all right, I
will be a flying cadet. If not, I will be in the air
corps, but classified as ground duty only.

Wishing you all happiness.

Bob

(15)
Aviation Cadet Center
San Antonio, Texas
Wednesday, 12:45 P.M.
12/9/42

Dear Folks,

Just received my fruitcake, radio and Bible this noon. They were all in fine condition. Thanks ever so much for sending them. I haven't tried the fruitcake yet, but I will tonight.

I received my cadet issue Monday. The issue included five pair of socks, 3 white handkerchiefs, three suits of summer underwear, 1 pair low shoes, 2 khaki sun tan shirts, two pants to match, garrison hat, service hat with wings as you will see in pictures I am sending, U.S. buttons and wings, air cadet insignias for shirtsleeves and coats, two pair white parade gloves, and two new suits of green coveralls. These clothes are in addition to what we received at Ft. Niagara. You can easily see that we are well supplied with clothes.

Yesterday we had out first open-post. We were allowed to go to San Antonio between the hours of 10 A.M. to 10 P.M. Buses picked us up here at the Camp and took us directly into the heart of San Antonio. We walked all over the city. We went through the Alamo. It is just as you see it in pictures. San Antonio is very pretty in spots, and in other sections it is really bad. One thing very noticeable is the narrowness of the streets. Main Street in Rochester is twice as wide as the widest street in San Antonio.

I had four pictures taken in a 5&10 for 15 cents. On the last picture I moved. I am sending them with this letter. I had a couple of pictures taken in front of the barracks by a friend. As soon as they are back I will send them home also. I haven't received notice of any pay yet. There is some talk about it though.

By the end of the week or the middle of the next we are leaving for pre-flight school. That is just the beginning.

It has been very chilly down here the last few days, but we don't have any snow here. How is the weather back home?

Your son, Bob

(16)
Aviation Cadet Center
San Antonio, Texas
Sunday, 12:10 P.M.
Dec. 20, 1942

Dear Folks,

You probably think that I completely forgot how to write, for I haven't written in 3 or 4 days. I have a good excuse, however. In the last 6 days, I've had two days of guard duty, three days of kitchen police, and one day of charge of quarters. Today is my first free day this week. To top it all off, they put my name on the kitchen police list again for this afternoon and tomorrow. I went over to the office and raised hell about it. They admitted that I had already done my share of details for this week and promptly took my name off the list.

Thanks a million, Norm, for the Christmas present. I was certainly surprised to receive two pair of socks and a tie. Every soldier can use all the ties and socks that he can get.

I received your letter, Dad, the other day. The day that I received Clayton's address, I sat down and wrote him a nice letter. I should be receiving an answer from him pretty soon.

Talking about food rationing, what are you going to do for gasoline, now that they have restricted all gasoline in the East? That letter you received from that Brig. Gen. was news to me. I guess it was a form letter they sent out to all the parents of Cadets.

I still have never received a letter from Dick. He will start writing now that he is in the Army. What every soldier wants above all is mail, and you have to write letters in order to receive any.

I received your Christmas card today and five others. I got one from Jo, one from Dorothy Lockwood that is Bill Stack's friend, one from a Mary E. Martin in Philadelphia whom I don't know, one from the Esker family and another from Harry Peso. I received one from Aunt Mamie this week also.

Give Glenn and Vivian my congratulations. It is too bad that I should have to miss both Christmas and their wedding, but if I make what I'm after it will be worth it.

A large shipment of fellows came in this week. They were all civilians. There were a number of fellows from Rochester.

I signed the payroll the other day. They say that we will be paid the 31st of December. That is good news anyhow.

What do you want for Christmas? Over in the P.X. they don't have anything that I feel like buying for presents. Besides, you will have to wait until after payday. I want to make sure of the amount of money I am going to have. They don't tell us how much money we would receive.

Love, Bob

(17)
Aviation Cadet Center
San Antonio, Texas
Saturday, 1:30 P.M. 12/5/42

Hello Folks,
I received my classification finally. I am classified as a pilot. There is a rumor around that we leave for pre-flight school in a week or two. We either will go to pre-flight school across the road to Kelly Field or else to California.

The weather is still swell down here. The day before yesterday it was pretty darn hot.

We are expecting an inspection by a colonel Monday, and because of this we have been pretty busy the last few days scrubbing out floors, washing windows, and policing the yards and surrounding area.

I went to my first picture show last night since I arrived here. It was "Me and My Gal", with Judy Garland and George Murphy. It was a swell picture.

My 15 days are up and now I'm allowed to leave my area and go to the show when I desire. We can't leave the camp yet, however, until we are given what they call an open post. On open post days we are allowed to leave the camp and go to San Antonio.

Thanks for Francis's address. I am going to write him a letter. I received a card from G. Granger the other day.

I am still waiting for the many things that I sent home for. I hope I am not troubling you too much, but they are things that I need and would like to have. I will let you know immediately when the packages arrive so that you won't wonder whether or not I got them.

Love, Bob

P.S. I almost forgot to mention the fact that I was glad to receive the clipping about Jim Ransom. He sure gets around doesn't he?

You don't have to worry about me. The way things look now, the war will be over before I'm ready for action.

I'll be in school for nearly a year yet if I don't wash out. About 60% of the fellows fail to make the grade. But it's worth trying for even if you do fail to make the grade. Our barracks are full of washed-out pilots. Most of them are reclassified as bombardiers or navigators. Some of these fellows have been monkeying around for over a year and they still intend to fool around another year. It is a great racket with some of these fellows. There is nothing like the air corps. You either die suddenly or live a hell of a long time. Washing out as a pilot is so common no one thinks anything of it. The fellows that learn to fly the fastest are the ones that make the grade. The fellows that wash out would most likely many times make the best pilots in the end, but at the present time the Army hasn't the time to train those who aren't quite as quick to learn as the others.

(18)
Aviation Cadet Center
San Antonio, Texas
Dec. 1, 1942

Dear Folks,
      Haven't received any mail from you in a long time. In fact I haven't received any yet with my new address on it from you. Are you receiving my letters?
      I received a card from Glen Granger today. It was addressed to Mitchell Field. I passed my medical perfectly. When I went back for my recheck, my blood pressure was perfectly normal.
      I should receive my classification any day now.
      Today our whole barracks was punished for cigarettes scattered around the yard. We have to march two hours extra at night. We marched one hour tonight. Tomorrow night we will march the other hour. It is fun and also good training.
      I had guard duty last night here for the first time. It is easy. We are on 24 hours. We start 2 PM and guard until 6 PM. Then we have eight hours off. Then we go on again at 2 AM in the morning and get off at 6 AM. We then have to stay in the guardhouse until 2 PM that afternoon. We spend this time either reading or sleeping.
      I hope you are sending me my camera and Bible. I also need my gym sneakers and my shower room slippers. They look like beach shoes. They are home someplace with the stuff I brought home from the YMCA. Gene knows what I mean.

Believe it or not, I also am in desperate need of some money. We had to buy our gym clothes here as Cadets which set us back $10.95. This left me pretty flat. We expect some money pretty soon, but we don't know when it will be. Either draw some out of my account or advance me some. Regardless, I will send it back home as soon as I receive a pay.

There is a rumor that we will start in school a pre-flight in two or three weeks. This last nine weeks after pre-flight we start flying school.

Allen Esker is sick here in the hospital. I don't know what is wrong with him. I doubt if it is too serious.

Have you heard from Francis yet? If you have, send me his address.

As ever, Bob

(19)
Aviation Cadet Center
San Antonio, Texas
Sunday 3:30 PM
12/3/42

Dear Folks,

I'm on guard duty tonight and tomorrow night. I don't go on duty until 6 o'clock, so I'm writing a few letters.

Lt. Gen. H. H. Arnold of the USA Air Corps reviewed us this morning and gave a short speech. I was standing only about 30 feet away from the reviewing stand and, therefore, had a very good view of him. He told us about our future, and also of what great importance the Air Corps was in this war. He was a fine talker and very interesting. There were 20,000 of us cadets standing there before him. He said he was surprised, for he was told there would be only about 9,000.

It is a fine day here. It is just like fall would be back home, only most everything here is green.

There is quite a bit of activity going on around here for they are leveling off about 100 acres of cactus and scrub trees to make room for 300 new barracks. It doesn't take them long to do it with the equipment they have.

Hope everything is fine with all of you.

Your son and brother, Bob

(20)
San Antonio, Texas
Tuesday 4:00 PM
12/15/42

Dear Folks,

Received your letter mailed the 12th in which you mention the camera and the Bible. Well, I have received everything. The shoes came today. Thanks for the fruitcake. It sure was good.

Well, our group wasn't shipped to pre-flight yesterday. We are here for another 4 1/2 weeks unless we are shipped to California. However, I believe there is very little chance of being shipped there. It isn't bad here so we don't mind too much.

Received a Christmas card from Aunt Mamie today. Glenn is certainly getting a break being home for Christmas. I wrote him a letter a week ago. I wonder if he ever received it?

I was certainly surprised to hear that you had received a letter from Uncle Clayton and that he was in the Navy. I'm going to drop him a line and see what he has to say.

Would you mail me Francis's address again and print it? I couldn't make it out before.

Dick and his mother certainly pulled a fast one didn't they? I wonder if he'll like it. It will be good for him.

I'm running out of words so I guess I'll close.

Your son, Bob

P.S. I'm enclosing some corporal stripes for Norman. Also thanks for the money. I was broke and didn't know how far off payday was.

(21)
Aviation Cadet Center
San Antonio, Texas
Saturday 7:00 PM
December 12, 1942

Hello Folks,
Just got out of the hospital this morning. They thought I had appendicitis, but I didn't. They gave me a blood count, but it showed that it wasn't appendicitis. Wednesday night I woke up with

severe cramps and couldn't sleep. In the morning I went to the dispensary and two doctors looked me over and asked me a lot of questions. One of the doctors was named Capt. Johnson. He said they would have to see that I got the best of care because my name was Johnson. They decided to send me to the hospital for a couple of days for observation. So an ambulance took me over to Kelly Field Hospital.

The doctors over there decided that it wasn't my appendix. The day I went in, four other fellows came into my ward for the same thing. I was the only one they didn't operate on. It wouldn't have bothered me if they had, for there is nothing to it here. It isn't as bad as having your tonsils out. They don't even put you to sleep. They give you a spinal injection, which turns your body numb from the lower part of your chest down. When the fellows were operated on they were only gone about 45 minutes and when they came back they were laughing and talking. The worst part of having your appendix out is the fact that you have to stay in bed 7 days before you can get up. They give a 10-day furlough with this operation.

After being in the hospital the second day, I decided that they ought to do something to me. I called the attention of the doctors to the cyst over my left eye. I told them it was getting larger and that I would have to have it removed. They agreed with me. Yesterday afternoon they took me in to the operating room, put me on the operating table and cut my cyst out. It took them about 15 minutes. They gave me shots of Novocain to numb the pain. Before the operation, they shaved my left eyebrow entirely off. I sure did look funny. The only pain that I felt was when they sewed it up. I am glad to get rid of the damn thing.

Received that money order for twenty-five dollars. I certainly didn't expect that much, but am glad now that you sent that much, for the pay they promised us before Christmas hasn't shown up. According to our Second Lieutenant today, they are not sure they'll received the money to pay us as they had promised. I presumed that the money came out of my bank account, but Gene didn't say. Nevertheless, I intend to replace it as soon as I receive a pay. I cashed the money order this noon.

I am sending a couple of pictures with this letter, they didn't turn out very good and I didn't have my dress coat on, so please don't take them up to the drug store. I will send some good ones as soon as my face is healed up. It is only a matter of a couple of weeks. Speaking of pictures, I don't have any of you all and I would like a nice one of each of you. You could send me those pictures as a Christmas present. There is nothing else that I would like better or need. Don't get me wrong, I don't expect any expensive pictures, just something inexpensive. You know.

I am glad to hear that Gene has such a good job and is buying as many bonds as he is. He won't regret it.

Tell that Norman that I am going to be pretty sore at him if he doesn't write me. He has only written me once since I left home. He had better get on the ball or hit the deck as we say in the Army. Perhaps he has too many girls to write to. Is that the reason? Well, anyhow, I am enclosing another trophy for him: a piece of stationery from a Texas hotel. Excuse the writing, but I am writing this letter on my lap. All the tables are occupied.

Allen Esker is out of the hospital and well. I was talking to him this afternoon.

Putting my clothes in the cedar chest was a good idea. That is the best place for them. How does Gene like his new room? The hours he is working doesn't give him too much chance to sleep in it.

Do you ever receive any letters from Bill Stark? I receive two letters a week from him at least. He is having an awful time. His weak knee is bothering him. It is all strapped up. He also is having trouble with his hearing. His commanding officer asked him what he was doing in the Army. He told him he was of no use in it.

Our barracks are loaded to capacity now. A large group of new fellows arrived here yesterday. I guess we are moving out Tuesday for school.

My back and hand are getting tired so I guess I will stop writing for tonight.

Your loving son and brother, Bob

(22)
Aviation Cadet Center
San Antonio, Texas
Thursday 6:30 PM
December 24, 1942

Dear Folks,
Here it is Christmas Eve, but it doesn't seem much like Christmas. In fact if it were not for the Christmas cards and gifts that I have received, it wouldn't seem much like Christmas at all. The

weather down here has been very hot the last few days.

We are still doing the same routine here every day. At 5:30 AM we rise. At 5:45 we fall out in the company street in front of the barracks for instructions and roll call. We go back in after about 5 to 10 minutes, make our beds, sweep and mop the floor, dust our lockers, window sills and lamp shades. Between 6 and 7 we are called out for chow. At 7:45 we fall out for an hour of body exercises. After this we do marching and drilling until 10:30. Between 11 and 12 we eat lunch. At 1 PM we fall out again for physical training. This time we play basketball, volleyball, or football. We come back in about 3 o'clock. Three days a week on Mon., Wed., and Friday we fall out at 3:30 for retreat. That is, we march down to the parade grounds and pass in revue by the officers of the cadet center. We eat between 5 and 6. We have the rest of the evening to ourselves. We either read, write or go to the show. At 9:30 lights are all out and we have to be in bed. Tomorrow we can sleep all day if we want to. It is a day off.

By the way, I received a package from Mrs. Stark full of cookies, candy and four apples. I thought it was very nice of her. Wishing all a Merry Christmas.

Love, Bob

(24)
Aviation Cadet Center
San Antonio, Texas
Friday, 1:30 PM
January 1, 1943

Dear Folks,

Today is New Year's Day, but yesterday was certainly a lucky day for me. In the first place, I secured myself a job over in the orderly room. It isn't a very important job, but it is a soft job. I'm dressed up all the time and I don't get K.P. or Guard duty any longer.

About an hour after I went on my new job, they sent me over to the supply house to get some express packages. When I got over there, I found out that one of the packages was for me. When I opened up the package and found that radio you all sent me for Xmas, I was so happy that I couldn't do anything but stare at it. Boy, but that is some Christmas present. I certainly didn't expect anything as elaborate as that, but I can't say that I'm sorry to receive it. I wish to thank you all from the bottom of my heart. You have made me about the happiest fellow in this classification center. I also wish to thank you, Gene, for that delicious box of candy. It arrived about an hour after the radio. Aunt Mary also sent me a 2-pound box of Fanny Farmer's candy. I wish you would thank the Grangers for me.

Aside from not being at home, I have had a wonderful Christmas. I received cards from almost everybody. Shirley Hanselton sent me a card and also a letter. I haven't answered her yet.

I received both your and Norman's letters today. From the both of them, I obtained a very good idea of what Glenn's wedding was like. He must have had a wonderful wedding.

You mentioned in the letter previous to the one today that Dad wanted me to mention the fact in my letters if I receive his letters. It was my belief that I had been doing this, but if I haven't I must apologize. I enjoy receiving your letters very much, Dad, as I do the letters from the rest of the family. Norman also writes a very interesting letter. He has a very good style. I received a letter from Uncle Clayton a few days ago. He told me the same as he did you, I guess.

They paid us yesterday, but they made a big mistake in the payroll and shortchanged all of us, so we turned the money back to them. We just wouldn't accept it. They promised us a new payroll in four days with our pay in full this time. They gave me $80.50 when I had about $112.00 coming according to my figures. It may be a little more or a little less, I don't know.

You asked for a picture for the piano, but I'm afraid you will have to wait about a few weeks until my eyebrow grows completely back. It is about a quarter of the way back now. Thanks once again for the wonderful Christmas presents and have a very Happy New Year.

Love, Bob

(25)
Aviation Cadet Center
San Antonio, Texas
Sunday 7:30 PM
January 10, 1943

Hello Folks,
       In this letter I am answering three letters. They are from Mom, Dad, and Gene. From your letters I gain the impression that you are really having winter and plenty of it. We have our cold days down here, but it doesn't snow - thank goodness!
       All of you mention the radio. I don't know if you received my letter of thank-you that I sent the moment I received the radio. You write as if you hadn't. I hope that you are receiving all of my letters. Anyhow, I wish to thank all of you again. It is the best present that I ever received. It was the best Christmas present in our barracks.
       I also received the candy that Gene and Grangers sent me. I believe, however, that I mentioned that in a letter before this. Please thank Grangers for me.
       Oh! Before I forget, thanks for the pictures you clipped out of the paper and sent me. I don't know whether you saw it or not, but there was a large picture in Life magazine a few weeks ago of us cadets listening to the General's speech.
       Bill Horrod wrote me that he was getting a furlough.

Gene shouldn't be too anxious to sign up, for once
he gets in, he will be in for a good long time.
Thanks a lot, Gene, for Jim Ransom's address.

Love, Bob

(26)
Aviation Cadet Center
San Antonio, Texas
Wednesday, January 13, 1943

Dear Gene,
	Well, they finally decided to pay us, and
today we were paid up in full.
	Enclosed you will find the $25 you so
generously sent me quite a while ago. By the way,
do you know where my bankbook is? I wish you
would look it up. I believe that by next payday,
which is only three weeks off, I'll send home a
chunk for you to bank for me. Let me know if you
do find it. If there is anything you would like or
would like to know about, let me know. How are
you coming along financially? Are you saving
some money?
	We expected to be shipped across the road
to pre-flight, but now we are not so certain. There
is a possibility of us going to a new school
someplace in Texas or even perhaps California.
	It has been raining here the last three days,
but this afternoon it cleared up and now it is hotter
than hell.
	We had an open post last Thursday and we
had a wonderful time. We went into the best hotel
and ordered $2 steak dinners. Later we went to a
skating rink and had a good two hours of ice-

skating. We finished off the day by going to a show.

Well, take good care of yourself, Gene.
Give my regards to all your girls.

Love, your brother Bob

1943 - Student Pilot Victory Field, Vernon, Texas
Dust storm forced us to head back to our field. On the way back to the field, my instructor did four consecutive slow rolls. Upon reaching the field, he made a power landing to control the plane in a high velocity windstorm.

1943 - Student Pilot at Enid, Oklahoma
Our instructor was a first lieutenant who had previously been a circus pilot. A superb pilot, but a daredevil. After 20 to 30 minutes of formal training, he would take over control of the plane and what a joy ride we would have.

1. Flying through train stations at platform level to wave at the waiting passengers.
2. Chasing horses and cows in pastures until farmers would come out with their shotguns firing at us;
3. Flying down country roads chasing traffic off of the roads, scaring the drivers half to death,
4. His favorite stunt was to fly just above ground level heading straight for a row of trees. At the last few seconds, he would flip the plane with the wings vertical to the ground and fly between a couple of trees. We had no choice but to go up and over the trees.

On my next to the last flight with him, I tightened the turn on the base leg of my landing pattern a little too much, causing my plane to shutter warning of a pending stall. I quickly dove the plane toward the ground to pick up speed and continue to make a perfect landing.

Upon landing, he took me aside and said that another student of his had gone into a stall and he had to take over to avoid a crash landing. He said that he had sworn that if that should happen again, he would wash the student out. He went on to say that since I have made such a rapid and perfect recovery that he would pass me for the graduation if I gave him a perfect flight the following day. The next day I gave what I thought was a darn good flight. Upon landing, he never said a word. I graduated and went on to twin engine school.

A month or so later, word came back that he was fined and grounded for a period for returning from a training flight with a student in the next class with 200 feet of telephone wire dangling from his struts.

(27)
Friday 4:00 PM
January 15, 1943

Dear Folks,

Just received your letters. Was very sorry to hear that King was killed. It seems as if all our dogs are killed by automobiles.

I knew that Bill wouldn't get married, for he told me in his last letter just before he left for his furlough that he wouldn't get married until after the war.

Headquarters just read off the shipping list for pre-flight this afternoon. Tomorrow we go across the road to pre-flight. And, boy, is it plenty tough over there. The first day will be a living hell. All day long, all that we will hear will be, "Pop to, Mister" (which means stand at attention and shove our chest out just as far as you can), "Stand in a brace, Mister" (which is the same only a little bit stiffer). "Wipe that smile off your face, Mister, suck in your gut, chest out, chin in, eyes front". We'll go through this and a thousand other cute tricks which they, our upper classmen, will think up. This will continue for four weeks and then at the end of that period, we will become upper classmen ourselves. We will have to know the Cadet Creed and the Air Corps song by heart. The cadet creed is as follows:

> My bearing is along a course directed toward the accomplishment of a high mission being to raise my earth born self into the blue above, to develop honor, self discipline and strength of character in myself so that when I am called upon to defend these principles, I will neither disgrace my country, myself, nor my honor. To this end I will strive diligently, honorably and hopefully.

Isn't bad, eh?

So Dick is in the cavalry instead of the Coastal Artillery? I thought he was going to enter officer's candidate school. I won't be surprised to hear that he likes it.

You will only hear from me about once a week or perhaps less for a while, for we don't have much time over in pre-flight for writing.

Well, I will say good-bye for now. I'll try to write in a day or so and let you know how things are coming along.

Love, Bob

(31)
Monday, January 18, 1943

Dear Folks,

Well, we arrived here at the pre-flight school Saturday morning.

You could never guess how really severe the place really is. Here they make boys into men and men into better men. When I say this place is rough, I mean it. The upper classmen live upstairs and we live down. But most of the time, they are downstairs getting us on the beam. Here is how it goes: They walk up to you and say, "Pop to, Mister." Pop to means to come to attention--a very severe form of attention. They say "Mister, suck that gut in. Chin down, Mister. Shoulders back. Arms down. Reach for suitcases, Mister. Heavy suitcases. Get those arms down. Suck that gut in, Mister. Did you hear me, Mister? You did! Then why don't you move? Sound off when I ask you something." Sounding off is shouting at the top of your voice. There are only three answers that a lower classman has for an upper classman. They are, "Yes, Sir", "No, Sir" and "No excuse, Sir". And let me tell you, they are always reminding us of that fact.

When you shout, "Yes, Sir!" or "No, Sir!" at the top of your voice, they will say, "Are you getting confident, Mister?" You say, "No, Sir!" Then they'll say, "Why don't you sound off, Mister? Sound off:!" "Mister, did I give you at ease?" "No, Sir!" "Well, stick that chest out, pull that gut in, pull those arms down, pull that chin down, head up. Mister, pull that gross gut in. Mister, did you eat much this noon?" "Yes, Sir!" "Well, you did? Pull that gut in, I don't want to see what you ate".

This goes on for a half-hour at times. They leave you for 5 minutes and come back again at you.

Incidentally, it so happens that I hold the center of attraction for I have the largest chest in the squadron. I'm not kidding or bragging, but for a fact I have the best look and biggest chest expansion in my barracks and, as far as we know, in the squadron. And are my upperclassmen proud of my chest. Chests are really important around here. They judge you by the size and shape of your chest. They have shown me off to every cadet officer and all the officers of the other barracks. They all agree that I have a fine chest. They haven't brought any other cadets around yet to disprove my reputation and they would if they could. I never knew that I did have such a chest, but it seems that when I stand at attention and suck in my gut, I am all chest and it really sticks out. They have me spotted as a future Cadet Officer when I become an upper classman. Chest means everything here to these fellows. I hope you don't think I'm bragging, but it is interesting and I thought you would like to know about it.

Our beds have to be made so perfectly that we use a ruler to measure the white collar and we don't sleep on our pillows, but put them on top of our lockers, for they have to be made up and the loose edges tucked in just right. We use rulers to measure off the spacing of the articles in our lockers and the size we fold our articles of clothing. The towels, socks, ties, and underwear we place in our lockers we don't use. We keep the articles we use in our barrack bags. It is too much trouble getting those articles on the shelves to use them.

I could go on for hours talking about this place, and how strict it is, but I haven't the time. It is wonderful. I love it.

School starts tomorrow. If you don't hear from me, don't worry. I'll be all right. Cadets don't have time to write. They get up at 5:30 and go to bed at 10. Every minute in-between is really taken up.

At the dining table, we sit on four inches of our chair at stiff attention when not eating. When you are at attention here, you always pick a point in the distance and stare at it. You don't move your eyeballs or your name is mud. While eating, you stare at your plate only. You bring your fork to your mouth and not your mouth to your fork. Upper classmen receive all the food on the table first. The lower classmen are last. After the first serving, before we can get another serving of anything, we have to shout out, "Gentlemen, do any of the upper classmen desire the potatoes or the meat, etc.?" They say "Help yourself, Mister." You say, "Thank you, Sir. Please pass the potatoes."

Love, Bob

P.S. My new address is on the back.
A/C ------------------------

S.A.A.C.C - AAFPS (Pilot), San Antonio, Texas,
18-1-D

(28)
Feb. 4, 1943
San Antonio, Texas

Dear Folks,

      Received your most welcomed letters. I am quite concerned over one matter though. On January 13th I was paid. I immediately sent a $25 money order and letter to Gene. However, I haven't heard from Gene nor have you mentioned receiving the money. Have you? I would like to know immediately, for I am worried about it.

      Another thing....all of us fellows have to pay income tax. We are going to have to fill out Income Tax returns. I can't fill mine out until I receive a record of what I earned at Redman's. Dad, will you please get that for me and send it to me as soon as possible.

      You will be surprised to hear that I was in the hospital 5 days with the flu. I am 100% now, however. I missed three exams and three classes. It was quite a setback, for we are studying algebra and we learn three or four new characters in code. Gene should be here, for we certainly learn the code here. We have learned the whole alphabet and are now on the numbers.

      By hard studying I caught up on all my homework and have made up all my exams but one which is an easy one on ground forces. In my math exam, which I made up, I got 95%.

We had our algebra exam Tuesday. I got 90%. I feel pretty good about that for I never had algebra before and I missed half the classes while in the hospital.

We are in our last quarter of math now, which is the study of navigation. Boy, do they throw the subjects at us here. You go through about 4 years of high school and a year of college in about 4 weeks. We had a test today in aircraft recognition. I don't know what I made in that yet, but I'm sure I did very well.

In about a week we'll become upperclassmen. Boy, does the time fly fast here.

I received a letter from Bill Horrod yesterday. He is in Louisiana and wants to try and make arrangements to see me. He might make it somehow.

I am very happy to hear that you got your fur coat, Mom. You deserve it.

I owe Uncle Clayton a letter, but I don't have the time anymore to write to everybody. I haven't written Bill Stark in 3 weeks. He'll think that I've forgotten about him. Tell Norman and Gene to try and see if they can't write a little more often.

Well, it's just about time to start studying again so I'll say good-bye for now. I'll write again Sunday. We have a day off then.

Don't forget to let me know about that money order and a record of my salary.

Love, Bob

(29)
Friday 6:00 PM
February 19, 1943

Dear Folks,

Well, that day finally arrived. I'm an upper classman now. We became upperclassmen officially on the 16th. We turned over red name tags in for blue ones. Instead of being the underdogs, we are now kings of the hill. Pre-flight School is on a hill, so it is referred to as "the hill" around here.

Our boys (the under classmen) arrived yesterday and boy are we giving them hell. You should see them, are they a big bunch of boys. They average about 6 feet. Most of us have to look up at them when we are making life as miserable as we can for them. Their size doesn't bother us. The bigger they are, the better we like it.

I made a 95% average in my underclass subjects. Our upper class subjects are right now: physics, ship recognition, and code. I passed 6 w.p.m. in code. I am pretty sure that I can pass 8 words, though. We only have to be able to take 8 w.p.m. to pass code here. However, if you can pass 10 w.p.m. then you are excused from code classes.

I'm receiving all your letters. I wish to thank you for writing me often. I really appreciate it. Your picture, Mom, is very good. I can hardly wait to receive the larger one. I wish I had one of Dad like that also. As upperclassmen, we get one open post a week. So I'll have my picture taken. I hope it turns out good. Our first open post will be this Sunday.

So, Dad, your job at Redman's gave out? Well, I'm certainly glad to hear that you went to work right away. I don't know how things are back home, but if you ever need some extra money for anything, you know where to get it. Don't be afraid to mention the fact if such a thing arises.

You've asked me if I'm allowed to play the radio several times. Well, as underclassmen, we could only play them on open hill days. Now as upperclassmen we can play them whenever we please.

You mentioned the fact that you heard that I had lost weight. I weighed myself today and I weigh 167 lbs and feel fit as a fiddle. I never felt so healthy in all my life. And as for worrying, I just don't have time to worry here. In the second place, there is nothing that I can find to worry about.

Aunt Thankful has written me several times, but as yet I haven't found time to answer her.

Did I ever tell you that Carl Leagey (probably spelled wrong) from East Rochester is here in the Pre-flight School? He also should have just become an upperclassman.

By the way, I'm going to send home "The Tale Spinner", which is our own paper. I wish you would read these and enjoy them and put them away in a safekeeping place for me. "The Tale Spinner" will give you an inside view of a lowly cadet's life.

I'm running out of words, so will say good-bye for now. I'm going to write more often from now on "I hope". In closing, you will find two name tags. The red one is one I wore as an underclassman.

The new blue one is what we wear as
upperclassmen. That is a way you can tell an upper
classman from a lower classman.

Love to all, Bob

(30)
Mar. 2, 1943

Dear Family,
Received your letters. Things are coming
along fine here. Received your picture, Mom. It is
swell. I have it on the top shelf of my locker.
Today is very windy and also very cold. It
seems like a typical fall day back home.
Last week we received instructions on how
to handle and field strip the Thompson Tommy
Gun. We fired it on the range Friday. Boy, that is
some gun. It is 45 caliber and has no kick
whatsoever. You can hold the butt on your chin
while firing it and never feel the worst for it. This
week we are studying the Colt 45 automatic. We go
on the range with that sometime this week. All
flying officers carry Colt 45's, so this is really an
important gun to us.
I had my picture taken. It is a good picture
except for the fact that I cocked my hat on my head
a little bit too much.
Received the Pittsford Post in the mail
today. Thanks for giving them my address.
Allen Esker is back. I saw him yesterday.
Received a letter from Uncle Clayton this
week. I haven't answered him yet, but I believe I
will tonight.

My school is coming along fine. I passed my course in the Recognition of Ships with an average of 99%. In my first test in physics, I got 94%. We have 2 more tests in physics coming up. Physics is pretty tough. I don't know how I'll make out in the next two tests. We are also studying maps, charts, and aerial photographs now. This is an interesting subject. I passed my 7 w.p.m. in code. I can pass 8 w.p.m which is all that we are required to take here. If I could pass a 10 w.p.m. test, I could be excused from code, but I don't seem to be able to do it as yet.

Love, Bob

(32)
Mar. 7, 1943

Dear Family,
Enclosed you will find my "income tax return" and a money order to cover it. Will you please turn it in for me? It has to be in by March 15.
Everything is coming along fine. My marks so far are better than those of my under class subjects. I got a 100% in my last physics test. I made 99% in my final test of Ship Recognition. Last Wednesday I passed an 8 w.p.m. test in code. We are studying blinker and will take a test in that sometime this week. Blinker is the same as code only it is done by a light instead of sound.
I have that picture I promised you. I hope you like it. I'm going to send it to you tomorrow. I had it tinted and they colored the eyes too blue.

When you see it you will realize what I mean. When you get it I wish you'd take it someplace and have the eyes fixed.

We went to the range today with the Colt Automatic 45-caliber model 1911. It is a beautiful gun. That is the gun all flying officers carry. I made 21 hits out of 25. Wasn't too bad for the first time.

Went to San Antonio Friday. Had a swell time. I went horseback riding for the first time. It sure was fun. Also went canoeing on the San Antonio River. I don't know why they call it a river. It is only about 5 feet deep on the average and 25 feet wide. It runs right straight through San Antonio. There are beautiful gardens and walks on each side along its entire length. When you get tired paddling, you can stick your paddle down to the bottom and shove yourself along. It was really fun.

It's time to study, so I guess I'll say so long for now.

Love, Bob

P.S. Ran the cross-country yesterday in 15 min. 28 sec.

(32A)
Mar. 14, 1943

Dear Folks,

Well, that day has finally arrived. I have finished Pre-Flight school. The final marks came out this afternoon. My final average for my upper class studies is 97%. I and another fellow named Kemp are tied with the honor of having the highest average in our flight. My average covering both upper and lower class subjects is 96%.

Saturday I passed the 10 w.p.m. test in code, which exempted me from the final 8 w.p.m. examination which was held this morning.

Excuse some of this writing for my hand is a little shaky. I was just doing a little Indian wrestling with a fellow named Homer Kelly. He is also from Rochester.

I went to church twice today. I have been going nearly every Sunday since I've been in the pre-flight school. It hasn't hurt me any. In fact, I believe it has done a lot for me.

It seems strange to have no studies this evening. After being so busy, it makes me restless not having any studies to worry about.

I'm going to mail home a candy box full of letters that I have collected. I'm also going to include that shell I promised Norman so long ago.

I purchased myself a footlocker. If you don't know what they are like, they are a small trunk. They are a lot nicer to ship your clothes around in than the duffel or barrack bags they issue us.

Well, I hope all of you are well and having a good time. I miss being home, but I don't get homesick for they keep us too busy to worry about

ourselves. Besides, I'm having a wonderful
experience.

                                        Love, Bob

(33)
Victory Field
Vernon, Texas

Dear Norm,
        I must say, that was certainly a swell letter
you wrote me. You don't write too often, but when
you do, you make up for the lost time.
        I am glad to hear that you are doing so well
in your Scouting. You just keep up that good work
and you will never be sorry. It develops leadership
and initiative in a young fellow. In the air corps
they think well of Boy Scouting, for they believe
scouting does a lot to help train the young into good
officers.
        I'm sorry to hear that your team didn't win,
but you came close to winning.
        You asked me for advice on what subjects to
take in high school. Well, Norm, if I were to start
to go to high school again, I would take a math
course along with a scientific course. Get all the
math and physics you can, you will never be sorry.
All your best jobs are involved in science and math.
That was my big mistake in not taking those
subjects. I hope that you won't make the same
mistake.
        When I wrote that your shell and a lot of
letters I have were being mailed home, I thought
that I would have time to mail them before I left for

primary school. However, I didn't get around to it. I did mail them this noon. In the box I put a 45-caliber shell that I fired from a Colt 45 automatic pistol. This is also the same shell we shot in the Thompson Sub-machine gun. I also included a lot of postcards from San Antonio and some swell cards from Pre-flight school. You can have all those cards from San Antonio, but I wish you would put those other cards in my picture album if you have time and if you don't, just put them away with the Tale Spinners. Show them around, but take care of them, for they mean a lot to me.

At the Pre-flight we weren't allowed to take pictures. But we can take all the pictures we want to here.

The presents for my birthday, they were swell and I thank all of you. The case of oranges was certainly delicious. At least all of the boys also thought so. They arrived here at Vernon field yesterday. Some of them were rotten, but most of them were O.K. We are not allowed to have any food here at all. We can't even keep candy bars in our lockers. So, please don't send me any more food. I'm glad in a way, for we get all the food we want here and it is the best. On the other hand, I hear that food is pretty well rationed back home

I haven't had my first ride yet. Yesterday, when we were supposed to go up, it rained. It also rained all day today. Some fellows did go up yesterday, before it rained. They said it was great.

I'm surprised to hear that Ken Dyer washed out. I thought that he would make the grade.

Well, I'm running out of words for the time being, so I'm going to start studying and stop writing.

Norm, I'm sending you a little present along with this letter. It's for two things: One for your birthday, which I let slip by, and second for being such a good Scout.

Your brother, Bob

(34)
San Antonio Aviation Cadet Center
San Antonio, Texas
Mar. 19, 1943

Dear Folks,
My bags are all packed and taken away. We leave in the morning for Primary. We are going to Vernon, Texas, which is about 40 miles from Oklahoma. The fellows here are on pins and needles, for this is the day we have all been looking forward to. At last we are going to learn to fly.
I received the cake and presents. Thanks, everyone. That is a swell clothes brush. I bought myself a new pen and as yet I haven't learned how to write with it.
Well, I don't know what else to say. I'll write as soon as I can and let you know how our trip goes.

Love, Bob

(34A)
San Antonio Aviation Cadet Center
San Antonio, Texas

Victory Field, Vernon, Texas
Mar. 22, 1943
Dear Folks,

Well, at last I'm going to start flying. We arrived here yesterday about noon. This primary school is like a dream. Our barracks are two-story tile brick buildings. We have hardwood floors, Venetian blinds with French windows. Our beds are 3/4 size with coil springs. We each have a large locker with drawers and doors which are kept locked. The barracks are beautiful inside, it is hard to explain. We also have a large beautiful bathroom painted white.

The food here is wonderful. We are fed cafeteria style.

The airfield is located 6 miles south of Vernon. Vernon is in northern Texas about 40 miles from Oklahoma.

Today we met our instructors. Each instructor has 5 cadets. My instructor seems to be a swell fellow. He told us that out of his last two classes everyone has made it. Here's hoping for our class.

Our planes are Fairchild PT-19's. They are a very nice plane. They are open cockpits. We are going up for the first time tomorrow morning. I hope I like it.

They wash out about 50% of their students here. Of course, different classes vary. That is what the average has been in the past.

Well, I'll write tomorrow and let you know how I like the air.

Love, Bob

P.S. We were issued leather jackets, helmets and goggles like those in the above pictures.

Bob at Flight School

(35)
San Antonio Aviation Cadet Center
San Antonio, Texas
March 30, 1943

Dear Folks,

I intended to write sooner, but I have been so busy flying and studying that I just let it slip by. So, to make up for lost time, I'll give you a brief summary of what has happened these last few days.

Saturday, Mar. 27

It has stopped raining. In the morning it is very poor due to a fog. We went on the Flight Line for the first time this afternoon. My name came last alphabetically, so I was the last one in our class to go up. When my turn finally came, I put on my chute, jumped into the plane, buckled my safety belt, and away we went down the runway. We went up to 4,000 feet. The view was wonderful, but the skyline was rather hazy. We could see across the Red River into Oklahoma. The instructor flew around showing me the different landmarks and auxiliary fields. We stayed up 38 min. This day has really made me grateful for reenlisting in the Air Corp., for there is nothing like flying. I love it.

Sunday, Mar. 28

Went on the flight line at 1:00 PM. Was last up again. After leaving the traffic pattern, the instructor gave me the controls and explained 90-degree, 180-degree, and 360-degree turns. At first I was inclined to let the nose drop, but did well after the first few. He then explained climbing and gliding turns. They aren't easy. In fact, flying an airplane is hard work. For a little recreation, he put the plane into a loop and then into a spin. He looked back to see how I took it, but I was laughing at him. For some reason, I feel perfectly at ease in an airplane. Nothing bothers me. It's just like floating. A few fellows get sick every time they go up. They just can't help it. We were up 52 minutes today.

<u>Monday, Mar. 29</u>
          We fly mornings this week. We took a bus out to an auxiliary field. We wasted a lot of time getting out there. I had a good day in the air. Practiced climbing and level turns. We were up about 5,000 feet. It was late so we came down the fast way. We dropped about 3,000 feet straight down in a spin. That was great fun. I was up 24 minutes.
          Today was clear but very windy. I went up second today. Practiced climbs and turns. Also flew along a road at 500 feet at a certain distance from the road. When they say 500 feet, they mean 500 feet. Very difficult to do. The wind was so strong that we had to fly at a 45-degree angle to the road to keep the proper distance from it. Your plane doesn't point in the direction in which you are going, but your path is that certain distance from the road. it looks like this:

```
                    ------------------          -------
-------------course



      _____
                                          road


      _____

   \wind
```

Received your letter, Dad. Was glad you wrote. So, food is hard to get back there? I guess that is because they are giving it all to us fellows. Down here, the people don't have to worry about gas despite the rationing. They all seem to have "C" cards. Tell Gene not to be in such a hurry to get into the Army for once you're in you're in for a long time. I know.

I'll let you in on a secret. Every time I go up in the air, I think of you. I know darn well if you were here, you could learn to fly the darn thing. Believe it or not, it gives me confidence in myself. I wouldn't be afraid to take off and land alone right now. I feel as if I could do it. However, they don't let us solo until we have 8-10 hours.

Well, it's almost time to go to bed, so I'll say good night.

Love, Bob

(36)
San Antonio Aviation Cadet Center
San Antonio. Texas

April 5, 1943
Vernon, Texas

Dear Folks,

I'm receiving your letters and appreciate them greatly.

So Uncle Clayton and Bill Stark have been around. I would like to have seen both of them. I have been corresponding with Uncle Clayton.

I suppose you would like to hear how my flying is coming along. Well, so far up to tonight I have 7:07 in the air. I have learned an awful lot in those 7 hours.

I've done spins, loops, taking off and landing and straight and level flight.
Believe it or not, but straight and level flight is the hardest of them all. One day you will do very good and the next day will be very poor.

Today, for instance, we practiced landings. My first 4 landings were perfect. The instructor told me at the time that they were exceptionally good for my number of hours. He said it was unusual. After he said this, I made four more landings and they were really lousy. That's the way it goes. I can do loops and spins with no trouble at all. They are a lot of fun. For a little relaxation, the instructor will roll the ship over and we'll fly along upside down for awhile. It's great fun hanging there upside down with your safety belt holding you in. In a few more hours we should start <u>soloing</u>.

Love, Bob

(37)
Victory Field A.A.F.F.T.D
Vernon, Texas
April 8, 1943

Dear Folks,

We are grounded today on account of rain. We sort of welcome a rainy day, for it gives us a chance to rest up. This learning to fly is all hard work.

I have been practicing landings and taking off the last three days. My landings are good. It's after I land that I run into all my trouble. I haven't learned how to keep that plane going straight down the runway. The darn thing will go one way or another, spin around and, once in a while, stall.

I stalled the plane once yesterday. I was so darn disgusted that I took off my helmet and asked the instructor if he thought I would ever learn. He said he wouldn't bother with me if he didn't think I could. That made me feel better. My flying isn't too bad otherwise. My landings are exceptionally good according to my instructor. My takeoffs aren't so good yet. However, I only have 8 hours in. We should solo in a few more hours. I'm ready to solo any time the instructor is ready to let me.

They are starting to wash us out in good numbers already. Every day my friends are being washed out. It's nothing against a fellow. You either can fly or can't fly the Army way. Anybody can fly, but everybody can't fly the Army way.

I'll consider myself a lucky boy if I make it. I'm trying my best, but if I don't make it, I'm going to take it in the right spirit.

You certainly are going into farming in a big way this year. I think Norman will make a good farmer. I bet he is looking forward to it. Ha-ha.

Thanks for C. Retchless' address. I'm going to drop him a line.

Love, Bob

(38)
Victory Field A.A.F.F.T.D.
Vernon, Texas
April 12, 1943

Dear Folks,
      I have some great news this time. I soloed today!
      We left Victory Field 8 A.M. this morning and flew to field #5 which is 15 miles from here. There, for 55 minutes, we practiced landings and takeoffs. Then the instructor, Mr. Gilfillan, taxied the plane over to a neutral zone and crawled out. he said, "take her up and make a good flight." After giving me what seemed like countless last words of advice, he said go ahead.
      I taxied the plan over to the end of the field, checked my instruments, opened the throttle and went roaring down the field. I climbed on up to 300 feet, leveled off, and made my first turn to the left, then opened up the throttle and climbed on up to 500 feet. The traffic pattern around an airfield is 500 feet. We can't break traffic and leave this pattern until we have made 5 solo hops.
      Coming in, I made a perfect three-point landing. I taxied over to the neutral zone and cut the motor. The instructor came over, shook my hand, and said, "It was a good flight." He then cranked the motor and said to take it up again. Coming in again I made a good landing. The instructor said I had made a good recovery from that one poor landing. They like to see good recoveries on poor landings. It shows that you have control of the plane and can handle it.

On dual practice landings, the instructor is always ruining your landings so that you will learn to recover from them.

I can't explain how it felt to take that ship up alone and know that you are the boss. It doesn't sound like me I know, but I wasn't the least bit excited. I felt just the same as if I was driving along in a car. Soloing gives you a sense of self satisfaction like you never had in your life before. Even if I wash out, I'll always have that much, which they can never take away from me and it really is a lot. Every day now I'll spend part of the time doing solo flights. I have 10 hr. 23 minutes in the air now.

Love, Bob

(39)
Victory Field A.A.F.F.T.D
Vernon, Texas
April 15, 1943

Dear Folks,

It is good hearing from you so often. Your letters help to shorten the distance that separates us. So, Gene is becoming quite a party man. He must be having some fun.

My flying is coming along pretty good. We didn't fly yesterday because of rain, but we did this morning. I flew solo again for 30 minutes. Every day now we fly first for about 40 minutes with our instructor and then he gets out and lets us fly solo for 30 minutes. It is great fun flying by yourself. It is a relief not hearing that chewing all the time from the back seat.

One of the fellows in my class washed out today. He has been sick every time he has gone up, so our instructor sent him up for an elimination ride today. The washing machine has really been running this week. Four or six fellows are washed each day.

Francis dropped me a card and said he was being shipped from California back east. I guess I'll have to drop him a line. Bill Horrod wrote me and said he was being shipped to California. He writes me quite often.

Say, by the way, did you ever receive that money order I sent for my income tax? I sent my income tax return and the money order for it, but you never let me know if you received it and paid it.

You asked me how I liked Vernon. I like it very much; it is much friendlier than San Antonio. The people treat us like kings here. San Antonio has been a soldier's town for years. Therefore, they don't have much use for any part of the Army.

Vernon has a population of 10,000. There are three motion picture shows, a cadet club and a country club to which we are all members. If we wish to play golf, they furnish the clubs.

I'm taking quite a few pictures here. As soon as I have some prints made, I'll send them home.

<u>April 16, 1943</u>

I didn't quite finish last night so here I am again.

I did some good flying today. I soloed for 40 minutes today. I kept taking off and landing. I make some beautiful landings. I dropped one in about 3 feet. It looked all right, but felt pretty rough.

I suppose Gene left today. Well, I'll say good bye for now.

Love, Bob

(41)
San Antonio Aviation Cadet Center
San Antonio, Texas
April 20, 1943

Dear Folks,

You finally have a flyer in the family. After four days of soloing around the field here, my instructor gave me a plane of my own yesterday.

When your instructor gives you permission to take a plane out away from the field, they are called solo ships.

I flew about 15 miles west of the field and practiced S turns, rectangular patterns, climbing turns, level turns, gliding turns, straight and level flight, etc. It is really great fun flying around out there by yourself. Altogether yesterday with my instructor and by myself, I flew 2 hours and 45 minutes. I was pretty tired last night from so much flying.

They are still washing the boys out in numbers here. We lost 7 Sunday and 3 yesterday. We are due to lose some more today. So far, they have washed out about 35% of our class. I keep my fingers crossed all the time. I can fly, but I'll have to fly the way the Army wants me to. They want precision flying and believe you me, it is pretty tough. I have 16 hrs. and 16 minutes of flying time in now.

Love, Bob

(42)
Victory Field A.A.F.F.T.D
Vernon, Texas
May 5, 1943

Dear Folks,

Sorry for not writing sooner, but I have been terribly busy lately.

We started night flying this week. I flew Monday night from 12 P.M. to 1:00 A.M. Boy, was I tired the next day. Flying at night is exhilarating. The air is really smooth at night. There is no bouncing around. All that we did was to take off, fly around the field and land for an hour. You have to land according to signal lights from the ground.

There are two long rows of flares between which you have to set your plane down. I did a good job for my instructor. He was pleased.

Because of a high wind and sandstorm, we are not flying today. I just got back from an hour in the "Link trainer". You know what they are. They teach you blind flying by instruments in them. This is my 4th hour of instruction in the Link. This instruction is only worth $25 an hour. That is what it costs in civilian life. So far, I've had a $100 dollars' worth.

They estimate that each one of us cadets that get through gets a $25,000 education. That is what it costs the government.

I have 40 hours in now. I only have 25 hours to go to finish up here. In about 2 1/2 weeks, if I'm still here, I'll graduate and be sent to Basic. If I get to Basic, my chances of getting my wings are great. Only about 10% wash out in Basic. So far we have lost 50% of our class here.

We are learning Chandelles, Lacy Eights, snap rolls, slow rolls, inverted flight, etc. now. Flying upside down is great fun. You have to lower your seat way down or else you'll hang out a mile.

Gene has written me twice. He sure is in a hell of a place. It's too bad that he didn't get into a camp that was settled.

I received a letter from Uncle Clayton today. He is in a radio school and he said he thought code would drive him batty.

Believe it or not, Dick finally wrote me. He is doing all right. He expects to be a Sgt. He is driving tanks, trucks, tank destroyers, and jeeps.

Did you receive the wings yet? The large one with the U.S.A. is for mother and the two small ones are for Dad and Norm. I thought the smaller ones would be nicer for coat lapels.

Love, Bob

(43)
Victory Field A.A.F.F.T.D.
Vernon, Texas
May 7, 1943

Dear Folks,

Received your letter today. Was glad to hear that you liked the pictures. They weren't too bad, but they could have been better. So you think I look older? I guess I do, but I don't feel too much older.

I'll have a large photo of myself in my flying helmet and jacket for you pretty soon. I hope it turns out good. It is the photo that will be in our class book. I've bought two class books: One for myself and one for you. Each graduating class here at Victory Field has one. They are swell.

I was the first one to go up with my instructor dual today. We fly about 10 miles west of the field and started our acrobatics. When we first got out there, we could see that there was a large sandstorm headed our way. In a few minutes it was coming pretty close, so my instructor headed back towards the field. Instead of flying back straight and level, he slow-rolled all the way back. In a slow roll, you just roll the plane over on its back until you are upside down and just keep on rolling until you're right side up again, all the time headed in the direction in which you wish to go.

Well, he did this all the way back to Victory Field. We must have rolled 40 or 50 times without stopping. By this time, the dust was all around us and we could barely see the field and hangars. You should have seen my instructor bring that plane in. He dove down for the field, leveled off about 50 feet, and then flew it in with power on doing about

90-100 miles an hour. We rolled right along the ground on the front wheels with the tail off the ground.

They are called two-wheel landings and should always be used in a high wind during a storm. If you attempt a three-point landing during such a storm, you're taking a great chance of cracking up.

Three cadets in solo ships during the storm couldn't make Victory Field. Two landed in #6 field - an auxiliary field to the east, and one landed in a farmer's wheat field. No one was hurt. The storm finished our flying for today.

Sorry to hear that Norm is sick. He had better hurry up and get well soon now that he's going to be a farmer.

Be on the lookout for a small package. I'm sending Dad his birthday present. It's kind of tardy, but I'm sure he'll sort of forgive me when he sees it.

Your son, Bob

(44)
Victory Field A.A.F.F.T.D.
Vernon, Texas
May 11, 1943

Dear Folks,

Your letter arrived today and I'm glad to hear that Norm is well again. I received his letter yesterday.

Sunday we were allowed to go in to Vernon between 8 A.M. and 4 P.M. to go to church. We didn't get any open post this week because 8 fellows stayed out all Saturday night the previous weekend when they weren't supposed to.

I went to the Methodist church with a bunch of the fellows. Since it was Mother's Day, the ladies at the church pinned a rose to each cadet's shirt. I wish to apologize for not sending you a Mother's Day card, but they didn't have any here at the Post, they wouldn't let us go to town Sat., and Sunday I tried to buy one at the drug store but they were all out of them. So, I guess I'll have to send you my love in this letter.

I know that Bill and Dick expect furloughs in June. As for me getting a furlough, it is as I told you before, it is an impossibility until I complete my training, which should be sometime in September. If I get one sooner, it is because I will have washed out. However, if I don't wash out and when I do get home, I'll have a pair of silver wings to show you. That is worth waiting for, isn't it?

We flew today for the first time in 4 days. It has been raining here like cats and dogs for 4 days. It gave us a chance to rest up, but we are behind in our flying time. We don't have too many flying days left here--about 9 days. We should be in Basic in 2 weeks. At least I can dream about it.

It's almost time for the lights to go out, so I'll have to say good-bye now.

Love, Bob

(44A)
Victory Field A.A.F.F.T.D
Vernon, Texas
May 13, 1943

Dear Folks,
 Just a line to let you know that I'm still struggling along.
 We are supposed to have our 65 hours in by this time next week, but we are behind on schedule because of bad weather. I have 48 hours in now. Yesterday I flew 4 1/2 hours in order to catch up some time. That is a lot of flying for one day.
 I didn't get any time in at all today on account of a low ceiling. The clouds were only 1,000 feet up.
 A girlfriend of Gene's who worked with him at Sampson's by the name of Margie Cook wrote me a letter some time ago. I answered her and today received another letter from her. She sent me a picture of Gene with a bunch of girls at the Factory. It is a good picture. Gene appears to be some lady-killer in that picture.

 Your loving son, Bob

(45)
Enid Army Flying School
Enid, Okla.
May 25, 1943

Dear Folks,
 We arrived here last night about 8:00 P.M. We left Victory Field yesterday noon by bus. Boy, those buses were nice, something like Greyhounds.

This Oklahoma is a nice state. We are northwest of Oklahoma City and most of the oil wells, I understand, are around Oklahoma City and east.

This is quite a place. Cadets from 4 Primary Schools come here.

The barracks are split up into rooms. There are 4 cadets to a room. I was fortunate. I got in the back room which is the nicest room in the barracks. There are three large windows in our room.

I'll have to finish this letter in pencil, for my pen just went dry and I haven't any ink. Our bags haven't arrived as yet.

We really get an airplane to fly here. They are Vultees with a 450 h.p. engine in them. The cockpits are just full of levers and instruments. The picture on the head of this stationery is a picture of a Vultee Basic Trainer.

I sent you 3 pictures of myself just before I left Victory Field. Will write more later.

Love, Bob

P.S. New address: Flight A-Barracks 5, Enid Army Air Field, Enid, Oklahoma

(46)
Enid Army flight School
Enid, Okla.
June 6, 1943

Dear Folks,
I soloed again Friday, but this time in a B.T. 15 after 5 hours of dual instruction. When you solo this airplane, you know that you soloed an airplane.

They cruise between 120 and 150 mph. They will do up to 300 mph nosing it down.

Once you learn to fly this B.T. 15, it is a simple matter to go to more powerful single-engine planes. After we leave here and go to Advance, some of us will go to single-engine schools and others to twin-engine. I don't care particularly which one they send me to if I can get through here.

They give us 70 hours of training here at Basic. In that time, we have to learn how to fly the plane, acrobatics, formation flying, instrument or blind flying, and night flying. During this course, we make a lot of cross-country hops both day and night.

We Link Trainer here almost every day. I'm getting so that I enjoy it.

I thought that I had a hedgehopping fool in Primary, but this instructor I have here takes first prize. He put me in the back seat after we shot landings Thursday and started off across the countryside approximately 2-3 feet off the ground. When we came to trees, we went between them if it was at the base of the tree and turn around it. Once, we went right down a road like an automobile, our wing just whizzing by the telephone poles. We did this for 40 minutes. It was the best ride I ever had.

So, Norman wanted one of those pictures. That's all right. I'm having more made. I'll send another one home.

Well, I'm pretty tired, so going to finish now. They keep us so busy here that we are all walking around dead tired.

Love to all, Bob

(47)
Enid Army flying School
Enid, Okla.
June 13, 1943

Dear Folks,

Well, here it is another weekend and also the third week that I have been here. I have six more weeks to go, I hope. I've got nearly 20 hours in here and expect my 10-hour check ride next week. If I pass that check ride, my chances of getting through here are great.

I've got a solo plane of my own now. The time really begins to pile up when you fly both solo and dual each day.

In another week we should start night flying in addition to day flying. That means less sleep.

The academics here are pretty tough. We get navigation, weather, radio, and various other subjects. So far I'm doing very well in them and am not studying.

We are starting to lose a few fellows in the washing machine. We expect to lose a lot more next week. The worst part is the fact that no one knows when his turn is coming.

So, Allen Esker washed out. The excuse he gives sounds rather funny to me. No one asks to wash out unless they're afraid of the plane or just don't like flying. Few fellows ask to wash out.

Gene writes real often. He writes me more often than I write to him. I don't have the time to write here like I did in primary. He sure has been in that hospital long enough, hasn't he?

I wish to thank you for the newspaper clippings. I find them very interesting. Those deer in Rochester certainly caused a lot of trouble.

So Francis is home. How did he get out of the Army? He is lucky.

Norman is certainly having a lot to do with the doctors lately. He had better get on the "Ball". By the way, talking about clothes, if Norman can use or wear any of my clothes, he is welcome to do so. They'll be waiting for me for a long time before I'll use them again.

Well, I can't think of anymore to say at the present, so I'll close now.

Love to all, Bob

(48)
Victory Field A.A.F.T.T.D
Vernon, Texas
June 24, 1943

Dear Folks,
Today was graduation day for our upper class. They leave today and tomorrow for Advance Schools. They only have 9 weeks to go in Advance and they get their wings. We have 13 weeks to go.

The graduation was really nice, just like Randolph Field. At the end of the exercise, 60 planes flew 100-feet over our heads in a beautiful formation. Moments like that really make one feel proud to be an Aviation Cadet.

Our under class men are supposed to arrive here Sunday. The past 4 1/2 weeks certainly have gone by fast.

I passed my 10-hour check Wednesday. This 20-hour check is a milestone. If you pass that, your chances are fairly good. We are doing instrument flying now. The instructor flies in the front seat while we sit on the back with a black hood over our canopy. The instructor gets the plane off the ground and up into the air. Then we take over and fly as he directs us. All you have to go by are your numerous instruments. Tough.

I made my first cross-country trip yesterday. I took off from the field here and flew to Anthony, Kansas. At Anthony we had to buzz the field a few feet off the ground and then come in for a landing. From Anthony, we flew to Blackwell, Oklahoma. We also landed here. We turned to Enid from Blackwell. The entire trip was only 150 miles. It took me one hour and 42 minutes for the entire trip.

We are supposed to get another cross-country Saturday.

Monday we start night flying. We also make night cross-country trips here.

Sorry to hear about you losing the horse. That certainly was tough luck. We always seem to have bad luck with animals.

You should be down here. The heat this last week has been terrific. The perspiration just rolls off in streams.

So Dick is home on a furlough. Lucky boy. Perhaps I'll get me one some day and not too far away.

Love, Bob

(49)
Victory Field A.A.F.T.T.D
Vernon, Texas
June 25, 1943

Dear Norman,

You certainly surprised me with that letter
of yours, but it was a real nice surprise. So you
went over to East Rochester and did some work for
Grandmother? That was swell and I'll bet she
really appreciated it. Since Dick is gone they must
have a hard time getting such things done.

You're getting to be a real bird lover, aren't
you? Do you study them in connection with your
Boy Scout work?

The ceiling was so low today that flying was
called off. We were supposed to fly a cross-country
trip too. We'll make the trip tomorrow morning if
the weather permits.
I'm sending you a sketch of the cross-country.
Perhaps you can look it up on a map.

The trip is 226 miles long and will take a
little over 2 hours to fly. We land and take right off
again at both Pratt and Waynoka.

We start our night flying tomorrow night. I
won't be able to make it though, for I'm having a
wisdom tooth pulled tomorrow afternoon and will
be grounded for 24 hours.

Love, Bob

(50)
Victory Field A.A.F.T.T.D
Vernon, Texas
July 9, 1943

Dear Folks,
      I'm sorry that I haven't written very often lately, but I hope you understand why. We are flying every other night and don't get to bed until 2 or 3 in the morning.
      The nights we fly we don't get up until 8 in the morning. Otherwise, we get up at 6 AM.
      Wednesday night, we flew a night cross-country of a hundred and twenty-six miles. Night navigation is easier than the day navigation. However, we had 2 fellows get lost. They each had to buy cokes for everyone in our flight. It cost them $3.50 each.
      We flew from Enid to Edmond, which are just a few miles north of Blazing lights. It really seems to be a large city. From Edmond we flew to Perry and back to Enid.
      I passed my instrument check, that is blind flight, and have made two blind flight cross-countries.
      On the blind flight cross-country, another student goes along as an observer. He takes the plane off and climbs it up to the specified altitude. Then you go under the hood in the back cockpit and fly the cross-country with only your instruments to guide you. If you are good, you can hit your checkpoints right on the nose and tell the fellow in the front cockpit when you are right over the top of it. These flights are usually about 100 miles long.
      On my first cross-country on the trip back to Enid, I told the observer that we should be here. He

answered back over the interphones for me to come out from under the hood. When I did, I couldn't see the field. I was a little worried until he banked the plane, and there right below us was the field.

I have 60 hours in here now and only have one more check ride to go. We leave here around the last of this month for Advance. We had our choice between going to fighter or bomber schools. I chose bomber. So next month I should be learning how to fly a two-engine plane.

Received your snapshots. They are swell. They certainly make me wish I was back home. I've been away from home a long time now....nine months.

I've lost track of Uncle Clayton. Do you have his new address? I like to keep in touch with him. Shirley Huselton wrote me some time ago, but as yet I haven't gotten around to answering her.

I'm enclosing those negatives at last. There are some there that I don't believe would interest her, but she can take her choice. Be sure you get the negatives back and save them for me.

Gene wrote me and said that he finally got out of the hospital. I'm glad of that. It's no fun in an Army hospital.

Well, that is about all I can think of to say right now.

Love, Bob

(51
Enid Army Flying School
Enid, Okla.
July 18, 1943

Dear Folks,
        Received your nice long letter yesterday.
It's great receiving your letters from home.
        I just came back from Open Post in Enid. I
bowled about 20 games and took in a show. I like
to bowl, but it is so warm down here that after
bowling a few games, you're soaked.
        I'm all done with my flying here except for
2 hours solo formation and my final check. This
coming week will be our last week of flying here.
We expect to go to Frederick, Oklahoma for our
Advance training.
        Do you hear from Bill Horrod? I've written
him, but he hasn't written to me since I've been
here in Enid.
        I'm glad that you liked my class book. We
are supposed to get some sort of a class book here,
but I don't know whether we will or not.
        I received a letter from Shirley Huselton this
week. She said that her mother has a new job in the
mill. She's in a machine shop. She doesn't run any
machinery, just hands out tools and fills oil cans.
Shirley said that her father still worked night and
day. I guess Shirley does the housework.

                            As ever, love, Bob

P.S. In this week's Life, there are a lot of pictures showing girls learning to fly Primary trainers and Basic trainers -- the same planes that we fly.

(52)
Enid Army Flying School
Enid, Okla.
July 21, 1943

Dear Folks,
        Your letter dated July 18 arrived today. Yes, I knew that my picture was in that group drilling. I wondered if you would find it. It wasn't very clear, I'm afraid.
        So, Carlton is a Sergeant Pilot? He may be a Sergeant, but I have my doubts about him being a pilot. Does he have any wings? Most likely he is a member of the ground crew.
        I can't understand why I never received those cards that Jean Wimple sent to me. She must have addressed them wrong, or else it seems as if they would have reached me.
        Very glad to hear that you are getting a new bedroom suit. You have needed it for a long time.
        I haven't heard from Gene in a week or more. When he was in the hospital, he wrote to me three or four times a week.
        We have our final examination in weather tomorrow. We had our final exams in code and blinker lamp Monday. This is our last week here.
        I also had my final check ride Monday. He didn't tell me, but I believe that I passed it O.K.
        We graduate this coming Tuesday and leave some time next week for Advance. All I have to do is to last nine weeks in Advance and I'm made.

Basic is supposed to be the toughest part. Advance isn't usually too difficult to get through.

Love, Bob

(53)
Enid Army Flying School
Enid, Okla.
July 25, 1943

Dear Folks,
I have another picture here for you. I hope that you like it. A friend of mine took it the day we left Primary. He just received the prints back from Eastman Kodak this week. The fellow in the picture is John Hillhouse. He had the same instructor as I did in Primary. He washed out here in Basic, though.

Well, we're all done here now. We graduate Tuesday and leave for Advance Thursday or Friday. We believe that we will be shipped to some Advance School here in Oklahoma.

Bill Stark is in Atlanta, Georgia now in a truck school. He claims that he has a good chance of becoming an instructor there.

What a heat wave we've had down here. It has been above 100 degrees Fahrenheit every day for over a week. It was 106 degrees for a couple of days.

I haven't received a letter from Gene in over a week. He must be pretty busy now. I'm also enclosing a picture from a magazine of some mechanics working on a B.T. 15.

You can see that it has a pretty good-sized motor.

Love, Bob

(54)
Enid Army Flying School
Enid, Okla.
July 30, 1943

Dear Folks,

Well, I arrived here yesterday around 6:30 PM. We came down from Enid on a train that stopped at every town it came to.

We graduated Tuesday at Enid. After graduation exercises were over, they gave our instructors and us a big blowout and in the evening, we had a big graduation dance in the Youngblood Hotel in Enid. Yesterday was graduation day here. When we arrived, all you could see were brand-new Second Lieutenants with their new gold bars and silver wings running all over the place. Only 4 out of 60 who were under the "flight officer act" were made flight officers. Flight officers received the same pay and wear the same clothes as Second Lieutenants, only their bars are blue and gold instead of gold and are a rank lower than a Second Lieutenant.

The flight officers' act went into effect July 15, 1942. It says that all cadets appointed after that date will be made flight officers unless they prove to be outstanding as officer material and leaders. Most of the fellows in my class come under this act. I do. One thing about being a flight officer is that you have less administrative responsibilities and yet receive the same pay and privileges. However, the way it looks, most of the fellows are still being made Lieutenants.

We live in tar papered barracks, but they are fairly decent inside. Food is good. This is a brand-new field and the class that graduated yesterday was the second class to graduate from here. Ours will be the fourth.

This afternoon we were issued flying suits and caps, a real good pair of sunglasses. These are ours for keeps if we graduate. We are also issued a brand-new parachute to keep.

For the first four and one-half weeks here, we are given an intensive ground school course. The last 4 1/2 weeks we don't have any ground school whatsoever.

The planes pictured on the letterhead are AT 17 made by Cessna and that is what we will fly here. I'm enclosing a picture postcard of some.

The way I understand it, our instructors will take us up for two rides and then let us go solo. But the way that you solo is for two cadets to go up together, one as pilot and the other as copilot. There are always two men in the plane. You are never allowed to go up alone. That's their method of training you to fly twin engine planes. We are supposed to get time in B25's our last 4 1/2 weeks here. Those are the planes that bombed Tokyo.

We won't start flying until about Tuesday.

Love, Bob

My new address,
        Av/C--------
        Cadet Detachment, Frederick Army Air
field, Frederick, Okla.

(55)
Victory Field A.A.F.F.T.D.
Vernon, Texas
August 15, 1943

Dear Folks,
        Your pictures are great. Very glad to
receive them. Whoever takes Norman's pictures
seems to always move the camera.
        If I thought I was busy at Primary and Basic,
I was only kidding myself. We put in a 17-hour day
here.
        They gave us 4 hours of dual and then sent
us to the instrument school here for two weeks. My
first solo ride was an instrument team ride under the
hood.
        Instrument flying is the most important
phase of our training here. If I pass my final
instrument check the last of next week, it will be
smooth sailing the rest of the way. We get up here
at 6 AM, go to ground school until 11:00 PM. That
is what you would call a pretty busy day. I fly at
least 3 hours a day plus 1-2 hours of Link. When
we start night flying, which will be 2-3 more hours
a day.
        Today being Sunday, I went to Vernon to
see my Primary instructor, but he wasn't in. I'm
going to try and see him next week.

Frederick is so small and dead that almost everyone here goes to Vernon and other towns on their weekends.

I like flying this airplane very much. I'm very glad that I took twin engines. I don't know what sort of plane I'll fly when I graduate. Whatever it is, I'll have to go to transitional training for a couple of months to learn how to fly it. After I graduate, my training goes on forever. Even in combat you keep studying and training.

So you're learning to ride a bicycle, Mom. Just be careful and don't spill yourself.

By the way, they are still sending the Pittsford Post to Vernon, Texas. Will you have Norman give them my new address.

No, I didn't know Wm. Briggs, but I have heard of him.

Don't get too excited about me getting a furlough. Part of the last graduating class got theirs and part didn't. But I'm going to try real hard. It all depends upon what sort of training they send us to after we graduate.

I have more mail to answer and I never seem to find time to answer it. I'm in a hell of a mess with my correspondence.

Love, Bob

(56)
Army Air Forces Advanced Flying School
Frederick, Oklahoma
Aug. 22, 1943
Sunday

Dear Folks,

I have just finished up the toughest two weeks that I've had since I started training. I passed my final instrument check ride yesterday. Training 17 hours a day was a little too much. I'm glad it is over with. After graduating, I should be able to get myself an instrument rating with a little more training.

I ordered my officer's clothes last week. The government gives us $250 with which to buy our uniforms. Then that just gives you the bare essentials. Our clothes are all tailored and should fit as if we were poured into them

Yesterday, three A-20's landed here at the field and I got myself in the pilot's seat. Boy, what an airplane. This one had 4 cannons plus two 50-caliber machine guns in its nose and two 50-caliber machine guns in a turret in back. Norman probably knows what an A-20 looks like.

Yes, I received the sewing kit. Thanks a lot. I've made good use of it already. My buttons are always falling off.

Say, does everyone we know work down at the shop where Dad is?

I received a letter from Bill this last week, the first one in over two months. He acts as if he has had his fill of the Army. I should be making some three and four-hundred-mile cross-country trips in a week or so.

Love, Bob

(59)
Enid Army Flying School
Enid, Okla.
Sept. 5, 1943

Dear Folks,

Sorry to hear about Aunt Mary being totally blind. Her family must feel pretty bad about it.

Well, only 26 days before graduation. Our upper class graduated last Monday. Most of them received 10-day furloughs, so I'm looking forward to getting one. Dick dropped me a card and said that he was getting a 15-day furlough and that he could get it at the first of October. Wouldn't it be great if we could both be home at the same time?

We are flying every other night now. Friday night we flew night formation. That is real tricky business. Today is Sunday, but we have to fly tonight.

Yesterday, instead of flying, we shot skeet all afternoon. I shot 75 rounds. We are required to shoot 300 rounds before graduating. It's great sport.

Our day flying is mostly cross-countries. They are usually around 400 miles long. We flew one down to Forth Worth and Dallas this week. The country down that way is really beautiful from the air. It's the only part of Texas that I've seen so far that I have liked.

Mrs. Cappette wrote me a letter and sent me some pictures of her and you. She also sent me a box with a lovely cake, candy, gum and marshmallows. It was all a big surprise to me. She must be a very nice person. She certainly didn't have to do that. I wish you would thank her very kindly for me.

I know that I should write more often, but there hardly seems to be anything to write about. I'll see if I can't find something to say and write more often.

Love, Bob

(60)
Enid Army Flying School
Enid, Okla.
Sept. 12, 1943

Dear Folks,

We are counting the days now, only 18 more before graduation.

Flying has been cut to every other day now because we are so far up on our time. We are still flying nights. We made a 360-mile cross-country Wednesday night, landing at Dallas, Texas en route. It is beautiful flying at night with a full moon and white fluffy clouds. One of my favorite pastimes is buzzing among the clouds.

The other night, a bad storm came up and two planes from San Marcus, Texas got lost up here in this part of Oklahoma and crashed. They found one plane, but not the other. The next day our Flight went on a searching party for the plane. We flew for three hours about 500 feet above the ground, but didn't find it. They probably found it in some other section. The two planes that crashed were navigation ships used to train Navigators.

Gene wrote me and told me all about his college life. It sounds pretty nice. He says that he likes it. I'm glad he does, for it is a lot better than the regular Army.

Dick wrote and said that he is getting a furlough on October 1st. Won't that be swell? If I get mine we'll be home together. According to the way Dick writes he certainly likes driving his tanks. The only thing that bothers him is that he doesn't see how he can gain weight by rattling around in a tank.

Love, Bob

(61)
Victory Field A.A.F.F.T.D
Vernon, Texas
Sept. 29, 1943

Dear Folks,

I suppose that by this time you have received the invitations and pictures that I sent you. I have had my reservation on a plane from Oklahoma City to Chicago confirmed. If I do get a leave, I should be home sometime Sunday, in all probability in the afternoon or evening.

We have turned in all our Cadet clothes except two suits of suntans, which we turn in the day we graduate.

We were issued a beautiful aviator's traveling bag and our winter flying clothes. They are all sheepskin. We have the boots, pants, jackets, and caps. When you get yourself all bundled up in them, they make you look and feel like a hot rock.

I'm a Second Lieutenant, but not officially until the morning of graduation. We wear our bars to graduation where we take the oath and receive our wings.

I do wish you all could be here for the graduation, but on the other hand, it would be difficult to get transportation out of here. Alone I can move faster and spend the most of my leave at home if I do get one.

Tomorrow I'll get my last Cadet pay. From then on, I'll make $225 a month clear. The only thing that will come out of my pay will be my insurance. That will cost me about $6.00 a month for $10,000 worth of insurance.

Hoping to see you all real soon.

Love, Bob

Going To War

Army Air Force Base - Clovis

When my graduation leave came to an end, I reported to the Army Air Force Base at Clovis, New Mexico for training on the B-24 Bomber. Coming face to face with the B-24 was awesome. It was huge in size compared to what I had been training on before graduation. Stepping into the cockpit, you were greeted with numerous controls and meters. I was in awe and completely spellbound.

I was assigned as copilot to a couple of pilots. After a couple of hours of flying time, I quickly memorized what every meter and control was for in the operation of this huge but beautiful airplane. On my third flight, I was assigned to fly as copilot to a short-in-stature pilot who told me that he had previously been a fighter pilot. On the take-off, he was OK, but on the landing he flew into the ground and bounced the plane with the nose pointed skyward. I had no choice but to grab the controls and to point the plane's nose toward the earth to avoid stalling. I then proceeded to make a perfect landing.

On the next take off, he performed in a perfectly acceptable fashion, but when it came time for a landing, he said to me, "you land it. You fly better than I do."

He would not attempt another landing. I learned later that he turned himself in and was taken off of flying duty.

In November 1943, I was assigned to the 400 Group 608 Squadron on Alamogordo, New Mexico. Here I trained numerous hours under the hood and flying strictly on instruments. Here I also met Walt Wenger and was assigned to him as copilot. He was a 1st Lieutenant having previously acquired quite a few flying hours towing targets on the West coast for gun practice for fighter planes. He was a very experienced pilot and we soon had a great deal of respect for each other. Walt was married to a beautiful girl by the name of Ruthie. He was the only married man in our crew.

We started night flight training. We took off shortly after dark and flew for 6 hours. Most of the nights were beautiful moonlit nights and the sky so clear that you could see for miles. After the end of a 6-hour flight, we were starved and, therefore, would head for the officer's dining hall that featured black iron stoves. We would order a half dozen fried eggs at a time and sometimes the second half dozen before our appetites were put to bed.

Our next training assignment was the AA Base in Charleston, S.C. from December 1943 to January 1944. We were assigned to the 6008 Squadron of the 400th Bomb Group. The Colonel in charge demanded tight formations and demanded that, upon landing, we were to land in as tight a fashion as possible.

We took his order literally and got in trouble on the approach of one of our landings. We hit the prop wash of the plane ahead of us and threw the wings of our plane in a vertical position. It took all of the strength of both Walt and I to get the plane in the correct landing position as we touched down for landing. Needless to say, if we hadn't been successful in muscling the plane back to the proper landing position, we would have crashed and gone up in flames.

I can't remember any more of our experiences here except that the entire group went on an overnight trip to Cuba. This was a most memorable trip. We arrived over Cuba in the afternoon and the beauty of the island was breathtaking, especially the colors of the foliage. We soon found out that we were on a whiskey run and we bought a case of whiskey for every crew member tax-free.

15th Air Force Base
Italy, 1944-45

      The plains around Foggia in southeastern Italy were the general base area for the 15th Air Force. A number of the airfields were actually constructed by the Germans, consisting of tents and flexible steel runways. Early operations of the 15th were conducted from Tunisia. The original six of the 15th Air Force bomb groups did not move into the Foggia area until around the final weeks of 1943.

      Our plane flew over from Africa and landed in Naples. Naples had become a shipping center for war material. The wharves were covered with tanks, trucks, ammunition, food stuffs, and all types of military hardware. My first day in Naples was spent with my crew getting acquainted with the city. Every place we went we were tailed by bands of ragged young boys soliciting business for their sisters and mothers. The young boys would shout at us with propositions regarding members of their family. This whole scene seemed really foreign to us Americans, but during wartime it was rugged living for these people.

Three days later we took off from Naples to join our new bomb group, the 454th , located in Cerrignola. Upon arriving at Cerrignola we circled the field and landed routinely. Young off-duty officers escorted us to a tent area where we were would live for the next six months. The tents were not yet erected, but we did not have to worry. The young officers proceeded to put up our tents for us and installed a stove in our tent. The stove consisted of a 55 gallon drum fed with gasoline from a tank outside. They also dug a slit trench for us to use in case of attack. We were elated by the welcome and attention we received and felt like kings. Subsequent crews did not get the kind of service and attention that we received as the first replacement crew for the 454th.

Our first bombing mission took place in late February. We were called out at 6:00 am for a briefing and were told our mission would be a short trip to the Anzio beachhead. Around 8:00 am, 50 B-24's took off for a low level bombing raid very close to the front lines. We were cautioned to be extremely accurate so as not to risk the lives of our troops. Sadly, the next day we were told that some of our bombs had drifted over our lines and killed several British officers and fighting men.

Squadron Group (Back Row: Bob, 8th from Right)

The next two days we made additional raids on the front lines in support of troops in the Anzio area. We doubled our accuracy efforts to prevent any further injury to allied troops. Subsequent missions were flown to strategic targets in Southern France and near The Balkans. Poor base facilities, inadequate fighter escorts, and weather limited the scope of these operations.

At the end of 1943, General Arnold made a number of changes in his air force commanders in Europe. Major General Nathan Twinings, formerly serving in the Pacific, moved to the 15th Air Force. During the period of December 1943 and January 1944, the 15th Air Force received its first reinforcements, six B-24 groups fresh from the USA.

The B-24 predominated in the 15th Air Force, as all but two of the fifteen groups diverted from the 8th Air Force would be so equipped. The B-24 proved to outperform the B-17 as it was designed. When in the hands of proficient pilots, the B-24 could equal and surpass the performance of the B-17.

<u>Combat</u>
<u>Vienna, Austria</u>

      On March 17, 1944, I was assigned to fly as copilot for a Captain leading the second wave of 12 planes for a bombing mission on Vienna, Austria.
      After takeoff, we headed on course to Vienna. Everything was normal, but it soon appeared that the Captain was having trouble maintaining the proper distance between the first wave of planes leading our group and our wave of planes. The Captain was overpowering our plane causing our wave to overtake the first wave, thus cutting power, causing our wave to fall too far behind. I then noticed beads of perspiration rolling down his face. He suddenly turned to me and said, "You will have to take over flying the lead because I can't." It was obvious that the Captain was having a nervous breakdown. I took over and immediately brought our wave of planes into proper formation with the first wave and held it there through the bomb run and the remainder of the mission.

Upon returning to our base field, I made a perfect landing. Upon getting out of the plane, I found the entire plane crew lined up to shake my hand and to thank me for saving the mission. The Captain never said a word but headed straight for the group headquarters where he gave me full credit for saving the mission. I should have received a medal, but I didn't.

Munich, Germany

June 9, 1944 - Raid on Munich included 500 B-24's and B-17's. Halfway to the target we lost the right outboard engine, which had to be feathered. To stay in formation, we dropped our bombs before the target and flew over to a group coming off of the target. The plane on which we chose to fly had another plane slide over the top of them and then settled down on the top of them causing both planes to break in two. This happened right off of our right wing. I had a bird's eye view of the pilot and copilot both fleeing the nose compartment of their plane as it broke away form the rest of the plane. We observed only three parachutes coming out of the two planes.

We had a serious struggle on the flight back to our home field in Cerignola, Italy. Our electrical system went haywire. Our pumps to transfer fuel malfunctioned. We had to transfer fuel by gravity. Other electrical systems malfunctioned. By the time we got back to base, I think they scrapped the plane. I remember Walt and I joking about stopping in to visit his Uncle Carl in Switzerland as we flew by.

We later learned that we lost 15 heavy bombers on this mission. It was reported that 40 enemy planes were shot down.

Ploesti, Romania

The most important target on our schedule was Ploesti in Romania, which accounted for 40% of the Germans' need for gasoline.

Indicative of the importance of this target was the frequency of which we bombed it. On June 23, 1944, we sent 400 bombers against it and 100 were shot down. On June 24, `944, we struck Ploesli with 335 B-24's and B-17's. On May 31 we sent in 480 B-24's and B-17's with large flights of P-38, P-47, and P-52 fighter escort.

Going into the target there were dogfights all over the sky between our fighters and German Focke-Wulfs and Messerchmidtts. One dogfight in particular was just ahead of our group and followed us into the target. The sky was full of enemy flak. As we closed in to our target, I glanced over my left shoulder and saw to my horror that our wing ship was on fire and turning right into us. I immediately nosed our plane down causing everyone in our plane who was not strapped down to ride to the ceiling of the plane and calling out, "What is going on in the cockpit....are you crazy?" I immediately put the plane back into formation and explained what had caused me to make such a maneuver without warning the crew. When they understood what had happened, they were too busy manning their stations to discuss it any further.

Bob and Crew (Bob, 2nd from Left in the Back Row)

B-24 Bombers over Polesti Oil Field

B-24 Bombers Going Back to Base

I Met My Guardian Angel
At 25,000 Feet Over Poland

On the morning of July 7, 1944, when we had been scheduled for a week of rest and relaxation on the Isle of Capri, we chose instead to fly on our 45th combat mission. We needed 50 missions to complete our tour of duty in the European Theater of Operations before being returned to the United States for a well-deserved rest. Many of the crew felt that we should keep flying missions and get our tour of duty done rather than take time off to rest in Capri. The crew voted and it was unanimous to keep flying. And why not? We had great confidence in the plane we were flying and in our own ability as experienced combat pilots. The B-24 was designed to fly high and fast over great distances carrying a large payload of bombs.

It was a beautiful, sunny day with hardly a cloud in the sky. Our long distance flight which began at 6:00 am. Our target was a synthetic oil refinery in the vicinity of Odertal, near the southwestern border of Poland.

The flight to the target went smoothly for my fellow pilot, Walt Wenger and I. We arrived at the target at high noon with no enemy in the sky. We made our bomb run and successfully dropped our bombs. Turning off the target, we felt a sudden shudder go through the left wing. We knew we had been hit as the whole plane began to shake violently. Looking out we observed a large hole in the left wing with shredded metal sticking up and gasoline pouring out. Almost immediately the same thing happened to our right wing. At that moment all four of our 1200-horsepower engines failed. Our plane was a brand new B24-J with a crew of 10 men. Walt and I were both rated as first pilots and shared first pilot time on our missions. We agreed that we had to abandon our B24 immediately before it caught fire and exploded.

On the intercom, I gave the order to abandon ship. We were informed that the ball gunner was wounded and that the waist gunners were strapping a parachute on him and throwing him out. The tail turret gunner was out of his turret and strapping on his parachute and gave word that they were all bailing out. In the meantime, our navigator, bombardier, flight navigator, and radio operator had already bailed out.

Walt and I made our way to the open bomb bay to bail out ourselves. There was a question in my mind as to how to do this. Should I go head first or feet first? I worried about hitting the bomb bay as I exited the plane. I finally dove safely head first and sailed out into deep space. We were at an altitude of approximately 25,000 feet and therefore, because of the lack of oxygen, had to make a delayed jump. I started counting 1000 one… 1000 two… and upon reaching 1000 seven, I passed out.

When I regained consciousness, I didn't know how far I had fallen, but I knew that I had to pull my ripcord in the event I should pass out again. So I pulled the cord and tossed it out into space...nothing happened! At that moment of great anguish, all I could think was that those dirty bastards back at the base had given me a bad chute. As you fall through space, there is not a sound, only a deep silence. I was busy wondering why my chute didn't open. Suddenly I heard a voice as clear as a bell. To this day I can only say it must have been the Good Lord. He told me to inspect my parachute to determine why it didn't inflate. I immediately discovered the handle to my ripcord dangling down below my right knee.

Evidently I had not pulled it out far enough to activate the chute. I grabbed it, gave it a huge yank, threw it away, and to my great relief the chute immediately opened.

I didn't know how high I was, and it was a long way to earth. I felt like I was standing still. Down below me I could still see our plane gliding to earth and crashing into a heavy forest. Before abandoning the plane, we had put the plane on auto pilot and, although all four engines were inoperable and gasoline was streaming out of them, amazingly it never caught fire until it hit the ground. When I got to within a few hundred feet of the earth, everything started going at a high speed. The ground was coming up very fast. We were trained to bend our knees in anticipation of the impact but I didn't. I landed stiff legged and was lucky not to get injured.

I was in a huge potato patch surrounded by dense woods. Quickly I dug a hole in the soft soil with my bare hands and buried my chute. I hurriedly took out my escape kit and opened it to check the contents. It included German money, maps of Europe, and water purifying tablets. I stowed it and started walking briskly down a path to the safety of the surrounding woods. Suddenly, I heard what sounded like pistol shots behind me and bullets began to whistle over my head.

Turning I spied two teenagers and a seventy-ish old man chasing me with pistol in hand. I stuck my arms in the air and surrendered. I wasn't afraid. After all, I had seen combat and faced death on a daily basis. I was, however, deeply disappointed at having to give up. Pilots always carried 45-caliber pistols, but this day for some reason I didn't have mine. Once again the Good Lord must have been watching over me, because if I had carried my pistol that day I might very well have done something foolish. The old man and boys were angry when they searched me for weapons. They had wanted that gun for a souvenir.

They walked me to a nearby highway and soon came a contingent of Lufwaffe troops. I was turned over to them. They marched me to a nearby village with thatched roofs. Curious villagers crowded around me laughing and pointing to the seat of my trousers that had split open, providing a full view of my bare buttocks.

Immediately a Gestapo agent came up to me and called me a "Luftgangster". He took off my field cap as he searched me and discovered a skull and crossbones insignia inside the folds. This skull insignia I had received back in training as a member of the squadron I was in.

I had forgotten all about it but it was all he needed to see to confirm my criminal status. He slapped me sharply with the hat several times and I felt the sting of the attached 2nd lieutenant bars on my face. Fortunately for me the Luftwaffe troops took charge or I would probably have suffered mightily at the hands of the Gestapo.

The Luftwaffe troops took me and placed me in the basement room of the local jail. It was a high ceiling bare room, with a straw mattress for a bed and one high small window. On the walls were eerie sketches of prisoners being executed in various scenes. This made me quite apprehensive about my future.

I was there for 2 days and then turned over to 4 guards carrying tommy guns. They escorted me to the train station where we boarded a private car just large enough to hold the guards and me. Shortly after the train started to move, all four guards fell asleep. I was sitting amongst my captors with a tommy gun poking me in the ribs. I reached over and gently pushed the barrel to one side.

Later one guard showed me pictures of his family. He had two young daughters, a beautiful wife and his mother. He said in broken English that they had all been killed in the fire bombing of Dresden. He must have seen the horrified look on my face because he told me not to worry. We were both soldiers only doing our duty.

The first train stop was at the Frankfurt station where we were to change trains. We got out and walked around until people in the station began to point and gesture at us. The guards became uneasy and took me to a lower level of the station to await the next train. Eventually I ended up somewhere near the Rhine River at a POW processing center. Here I was brought before a German Major in a large, well-appointed office. He asked me my name and organization. I responded with the standard name, rank, and serial number.

In perfect English he spoke to me. "Mr. Johnson, you would have made a fine looking German officer with your blonde hair and blue eyes. Now, you have to tell me more than your name, rank, and serial number. I like you and I want to get you off to one of our better POW camps."

I persisted with name rank and serial number and he ordered his guard to take me out. "I'll see you tomorrow and we will talk some more." I went back to my small cell with no windows to await my next session with the major.

The following day I was delivered once again to the German Major's office. I stuck with name, rank, and serial number to all of his questions and he finally said to me, "Mr. Johnson, I am not going to take any more time with you. I already know everything I need to know about your group." With that he pulled out a large black book from his desk with the title "454 Bomb Group" emblazoned on the cover. It contained very detailed information about my group. I was stunned and disheartened to see how much they knew about the 454.

The following day I was placed on a train and transported to the German Prisoner of War Camp called Stalag Luft III in Sagan, Poland. Here I spent the next 10 1/2 months as a prisoner of war until we were forced to evacuate the camp in the middle of winter.

One added sad note about the crash. I later learned that the ball gunner was dead from his wounds when he was found. The tail gunner was found in our plane wreckage. Apparently he didn't jump with the rest of the crew and rode the plane down. Subsequently I was awarded a Purple Heart for flak wounds received when the plane was shot down.

HEADQUARTERS ARMY SERVICE FORCES
OFFICE OF THE PROVOST MARSHAL GENERAL
WASHINGTON 25, D. C.

fld

11 August 1944

RE: 2nd Lt. Robert G. Johnson,
United States Prisoner of War,
Camp Unstated, Germany.

Mr. Leslie S. Johnson,
French Road,
Pittsford, New York.

Dear Mr. Johnson:

The Provost Marshal General has directed me to supplement the information you received recently concerning the above-named prisoner of war.

Information has been received which indicates that he is now interned as a prisoner of war as indicated above. The report received did not give the place of his internment. Past experience indicates that one to three months is the normal time required for this office to receive that information.

Until the exact place of his internment is known, it is impossible to direct letters and parcels to him. Mailing instructions and parcel labels will be forwarded, without application on your part, when his internment address is received.

Sincerely yours,

Howard F. Bresee

Howard F. Bresee,
Colonel, C.M.P.,
Assistant Director,
Prisoner of War Division.

Incl.
Information Circular

Prisoner of War Letter

Name: Johnson

Vorname: Robert O.

Dienstgrad 2. Lt.

Erk.-Marke 6667   Krgsgeflg.d.Lw.3

Serv.-Nr.: O - 693 990

Nationalität: U.S.A.

Baracke:

Bob, Prisoner of War

A Time To Survive

Stalag Luft III

  I arrived at Stalag Luft III in the middle of July aboard a train with about 25 other prisoners, mostly American and some British. The train passed through the main gates and we disembarked into a receiving area. We were deloused, showered, and given clean clothing. The clothing consisted of mostly British uniforms probably shipped in from Switzerland by the Red Cross. It was a real morale booster to be clean and wearing fresh clothes.

  We were called outdoors at least 2 times a day for a body count in all kinds of weather. If there was an escape attempt, we also had to fall out for a body count. Stalag Luft 3 was the camp where the famous Great Escape had occurred several months earlier and 50 poor souls had been executed by the Germans. Security was extremely tight when I arrived, but some die-hards were still attempting to escape. Our barracks were constantly being searched by ferrets, German soldiers whose job was to search under buildings for possible escape activities.

  The barracks themselves were long and divided into sections by bunk beds where 8-12 men lived together. Initially the bunks were doubles but became triples as more and more prisoners arrived. Every other week we received a shower. Toilet facilities consisted of rows of outside one-holers. We avoided going out to use them during the night as we worried about being mistaken for an escaping prisoner.

We received food rations and each small group took their turn preparing food in the stone lobby on an iron stove. We became pretty adept at preparing savory meals from very limited supplies. Cooking activities became an important part of relieving our incredibly dull daily routine.

Many of our officers were college grads and offered daily classes in such things as English, German, and Math. This kept our minds occupied and off of the dangerous occupation of planning escapes. Groups of men were always putting on shows for entertainment, and a shipment of recreational equipment arrived from the Red Cross and included such things as baseballs, footballs, hockey sticks, and ice skates. We organized games with this equipment and it provided a nice outlet for us. Believe it or not, I even learned to play bridge while a POW and we played every day. And so time passed and we became like family. We had to, to keep our sanity!

The Death March

While I was a POW, I kept a journal of events. I used scraps from things like cigarette pack papers to write down my diary and it is amazing that all of it survived the war with me. When we were on the move, I hid my diary inside the lining of my clothing and also in my shoes. I was often searched by the Germans but by the hand of God they always seemed to miss it. One time when I was searched, the guard found some Deutchmarks in my coat lining. He cussed and threw them on the ground in disgust.

That diary follows. In the beginning of January, my entries were pretty routine, but more details were added as time progressed. (Commentary added later is in parentheses)

January 1   Ate 3 good meals today. Spam and potatoes for breakfast.

January 5   Last evening, two men hit the fence and made it. Two others tried but were caught in compound.

January 6   Saturday morning inspection. Spent
               most of the day reading in the
               reference library in the combine.

January 7   Attended church services

January 8   Light snow in the morning. Studied
               German in the afternoon. Attended
               New Year's Day concert show in the
theater.

January 9   No appetite this morning. Didn't get
               up until 10 AM.

January 10   McArther returned from hospital

January 11   Weather much warmer. Rained
               lightly. Night German class. Blount
               received first personal parcel.

January 12   Picture parade at morning Appell.
               We are experiencing a heavy thaw,
               Skating rink has turned into a pond.
               I finished reading Oliver Twist.

January 13   Saturday morning inspection at 11
               AM as usual. Blount received a
               cigarette parcel.

January 14	Sunday Morning 11 AM Appell. The day is cold but clear. Hockey game between North and South compounds. South won. Joe Davis lectured on George Washington.
January 15	Very cold all day. Played four games of bridge after supper.
January 16	Very cold morning. Snow crunching underfoot. Helped to start fire this morning. German class 11-12 AM. Found worms in our barley soup at noon, but no one seemed to mind. Air raid alarm at 1:20 PM. All clear at 1:45 PM. Bombs could be heard in the distance. Russian front is moving towards us. Morale here is increasing daily. Just after lights out tonight, heavy bombing could be heard in the Southwest and flecks of light could be seen.
January 17	Very cold and strong winds this morning. Plenty of exciting news today. Russians on German border in two places. Tonight an Appell--it was that we would go on one Red Cross parcel starting Monday.

January 18	Cold weather. We received five Christmas parcels: four English and one American.
January 19	Still cold and the wind increased in velocity. Russians in Litzmanstadt. Warsaw evacuated.
January 21	Fair but cold. Hockey game which our block won. Tonight Col. D. T. Spivey gave orders for us to be ready to leave at a moment's notice. Colonel inspected to determine if each man had the desired articles. Starting tomorrow, each man to walk perimeter three times. To be increased to six times within two weeks. Russians still advancing. German planes of all types including gliders coming from the East have been passing over constantly these last few days.
January 22	Our blanket rolls were inspected at 1 PM. We were told that from here on out all orders would be written and must be obeyed without question.

Colonel Spivey emphasized that strict discipline was necessary. I'm sick to my stomach. I couldn't sleep well most of the night.

January 23   Snowed most of the morning. German class 11-12 noon. We didn't receive our regular bread ration. Today the Germans came in and loaded all of the bread on a truck and took it out. Looks as if our bread supply is kaput.

January 24   Bread came in today but the bread ration decreased considerably. FW190s and Me109s passing over a treetop level all day.

January 25   No German class today. Ceiling low and visibility bad. FW-190s, Me109s, Ju52s and Stukas filled the sky low overhead most of the afternoon. The Luftwaffe apparently is doggedly attempting to check the great Red Machine which, for the past week and a half, has been rolling across the Polish border into Germany on its way to Berlin.

Tonight the Russians are on the Oder only 45 miles from us here at Sagan. We were placed on a coal ration today. Wrote a letter to home. Doubt that it will leave Germany for a long time.

January 26   Russians make big gains in East Russia. No big moves toward us.

(Let me add here that we were all elated at the Russian advance. We gave little thought to what might lie ahead. Had we known what was about to happen, we would have been much more somber. Things changed dramatically on January 27th.)

January 27   Heavy snow last night. Overcast, but much warmer. Russians made big gain in West Prussia. Fighting in the streets of Breslau. At 9 PM we were alerted to leave camp at 11:15 PM.

The place turned into a madhouse. Everybody making blanket rolls. We tore up the benches and shelves to make sleds.

(We were all both excited and scared. Only God knew what lie ahead for some two thousand prisoners.)

January 28   Marched out of the main gate at 5:30 AM. Received one Red Cross parcel per man. The Vorlager (camp entrance) was covered with parcels stripped of prunes, sugar and D bars. (The rest had to be left behind.)

Left Stalag Luft III at 6:30 AM. Marched through Hermsdorf at 8:30 AM. Next town was Hammerfield, which is being evacuated of its civilians. Entered Hablau at 12:30 PM. Pole and French workers passed out coffee and bread. We stood in the main street for about three hours.

We were 16 kilometers from Sagan. Bitter cold all day. Snowed quite a bit. Spent the night here in a church. Sleeping was next to impossible. Ernie and I wrapped ourselves in blankets and overcoats and attempted to sleep on the floor in a cramped position beneath the seat of a small pew. This gave us some protection form the rampant puking going on.

(The majority of the men were ill with stomach upset and bad colds. Others were puking because of fear of what might happen next. Years later I revisited that same church during a reunion under completely different circumstances. We were met by the people of the church carrying flowers and were warmly greeted. My fellow POW's and I left cash donations that day to show our appreciation for the support we had received from the locals during the march long ago.)

January 29   Departed from Hablau at 9 AM and
              continued our march through
              Germany in the coldest weather
              we've experienced this winter.
              General Vanaman and the Colonel
              are still leading us. Admiration (for
              them) is increasing daily. Came to
              Freiwaldau, a medium-sized city
              situated on a hill. No trading was
              allowed with the civilians because
              the day before POWs had caused
              some trouble. Eight kilometers from
              Freiwaldau, part of the men were put
              into a large barn by the roadside.
              The rest of us continued to a small
              village. Spent the night in a large
              barn full of straw. We were in like
              sardines, but it was warm and dry.
              Outside of a few hot potatoes and
              some hot water furnished by the
              civilians, the Germans have made no
              arrangement for feeding us yet. Our
              guards are all old men with only one
              officer in charge, a Haupmann. The
              higher German officers seem to have
              deserted us. We marched 19
              kilometers today.

January 30	We are staying here today. Stood Appell (roll call) in stable yard. Spivey said that the Germans had a little food for us, but we wouldn't receive it until the food we brought with us was gone. Leveled half of the hay in the barn so that we would have better sleeping arrangement. Dutch and I walked into the home of a Polish family. They took us into their living room and let us take off our shoes and stockings and dried them before the fire. They fed us hot coffee and potatoes.
January 31	Marched out of Selingersruhr at 7:30 AM. Not as cold as yesterday. Snowed for a while. Entered Priebus 10:30 AM. We were asked by the Colonel if anyone has found a pistol lost by one of our guards. Entered Muskau at 4:30 PM after marching 28 kilometers of hilly country. (Needless to say , many men were suffering from cold wet feet and frostbite.)

Tonight we slept in a pottery factory
and have hot, running water, lights,
and heat. The place is very dirty.

NOTE: It was reported that when General
Vanaman joined us at Stalag Luft II, that he had
parachuted out behind German lines to be captured
by the Germans so that he could become a prisoner
of Stalag Luft III. Before the war, he had been
active in Berlin and had become acquainted with the
top Germans. It is believed that it was felt that his
current presence with the American POWs would
provide them with some sense of safety.

On February 1, General Vanaman again talked the
Germans into letting us spend the day here. We
cleaned up and ate a small amount of food. Men
from the West camp and Balaria came to the
factory. Their feet were frozen and blue. They
were in terrible shape. They had walked all the way
with no stops! Many of them were in serious shape.

February 1   Had a good night's sleep. Plenty of
               running water and heat. Workers
               here in factory are mostly French
               POWs. There are also many Italians
               and some Russian girls.

February 2   Up at 8 AM today. Prepared
               ourselves to march with one hour's
               notice. Weather has cleared and sun
               is out. This is my brother Norman's
               birthday today.

February 3   We awoke at 4:30 AM. It was
               raining and thawing. From here we
               went into Muskau. Because I ate too
               much margarine, I came awake at 3
               AM this morning very ill to my
               stomach and vomited five times
               before it was time to leave. We
               walked 18 Kilometers to Graustain
               and arrived at 2:30 in the afternoon
               where we bedded down in the barn
               with straw on the floor. For warmth
               we bundled two or three of us
               together. My feet are killing me.
               Stayed in barn tonight with 130 men.
               We had lights, hot water, and good,
               clean straw. We took turns cooking
               on stove in farmhouse belonging to a
               nice German family. We decided to
               abandon the sled.

February 4   At 6:00 AM we woke up and packed.
We left at 7:30 AM for Spremberg.
Along the road we met a lot of
Wehrmacht with shovels. We
entered at 9:30 AM and went directly
to a Wehrmacht transportation
school. At noon they fed us barley
soup.   At 3:30 PM we walked 3
kilometers and were loaded into
some old French, Italian, and
Netherlands boxcars -- fifty men per
boxcar plus two guards. We had a
cramped, miserable sleepless night.
There was barely room to sit down
and we had to take turns kneeling. It
was so crowded that if you fell
asleep, you would wake up with men
laying across you so that you
couldn't even move. It was
miserable. We traveled
approximately 40 kilometers that
night. Rumors had it that we were
going to Hamburg. We were very
thirsty, but the Germans gave us no
water.

The majority of men had loose bowels and were throwing up. That evening, we marched throughout the town to the marshaling yards. Here we entered a scene more similar to home with signs advertising Mobil Oil, Shell, Standard Oil, Kodak and others. They also brought in a Red Cross parcel for each man.

February 5   We arrived at Rutland at 11 AM; Muchenberg at 4:30 PM. We made very little progress all day, but that evening we made good time. We arrived in Dresden about midnight where there were lots of German troops going to the Russian front near Berlin. In Chemnitz, we were almost in the middle of an air raid. They locked us in the boxcar when the sirens blew and then the train took off like a bat out of hell.

February 6   We arrived at Zwickau at dawn and the Germans finally gave us water and German coffee. All the men were sick by now and were having bowel movements all over the place. Picture a line of men up to one mile long squatting along the tracks relieving themselves. Civilians living along the tracks were peeved and screaming to high heaven. We made better time after Zwickau. The Germans would not give us any water. We went through another air raid. We could hear planes over Netzschkau at 10:35 AM; Plauen at 12:15 PM. There were terrific bombing damages. We could see the forts and liberators this time.

February 7   We are traveling in extreme discomfort. We are filthy and cramped and thirsty as hell. Arrived at Augsburg at 7:30 AM. Finally, we arrived in Munich and we were put into a railroad yard which was really bombed out. We saw American POWs repairing it. We got so thirsty that we got some steam water out of the locomotive. Heard a vicious rumor that the war was over. Arrived at Moosburg at 3:00 PM.

Here we were placed in Stalag 7A. We went to the North Lager, which became known as the "Snake Pit". They put 600 of us in there without beds or fuel or anything. We were all sick by this time. It was cold and damp and everyone was covered with fleas and lice. Morale had hit rock bottom and many didn't think that they would come out of this experience alive. There was no heat or food. We are in a small reception lager where we spent the night in four small buildings like so many sardines. There was not enough room to have everyone lay down at once and many did not sleep, but I was so tired that I passed out and slept like a baby all night.

February 8-10   We stayed in the "Snake Pit". I used a blanket and slung a hammock and got some sleep. Everyone was really sick.

February 8   Arose at 7:30 AM Apell at 8:00 AM. We are guarded by the Wehrmacht and they seem more businesslike. An English Sergeant's orchestra played for us this afternoon.

February 9   Over 300 sick men last night.
               Probably caused by the cold, greasy
               food we have been eating for the past
               several weeks. Ill to my stomach all
               day. Under doctor's orders, I didn't
               eat all day. Germans brought in a
               boiler for hot water. McArther has
               taken ill and was put into a sick bay.
               All of the other boys and all of block
               51 and part of block 52 left for the
               compound.

February 10   Awoke at 7:15 AM. My stomach
               has straightened out. I feel like
               eating again.

February 11   After supper, we went through a
               search, which was a farce. The
               German searching me found some
               Reichsmarks that I had hidden in the
               lining of my leather flight jacket.
               After he had cut the lining and
               looked over the marks, he threw
               them back at me. Needless to say, he
               was quite irritated. Along the way,
               we had picked up maps, hammers,
               saws, nails, wrenches, and
               everything else that we had found,
               especially at the brick factory at
               Muskau. We left here about 2:00

PM and proceeded to the main lager where we filled out our change-of-address cards. From here we went to the showers and delousing chambers. After two weeks of dirt and filth, we finally became new men both in appearance and morale. We were placed in a very small compound with 200 men in each block. Our bunks are 3 high in confines of 12 with barely room to walk between. The beds had straw mattresses and were full of lice, fleas, and bedbugs. We took one mattress off a bed and counted over 100 bedbugs on the mattress. No locker or shelves of any sort. Being located in a top bunk, I've suspended everything from the ceiling. Our cooking facilities are nil due to the lack of fuel for the stoves.

February 12   Made a margarine burner out of tin cans in order to heat brew water and to cook what food we have. We have a huge supply of bedbugs and lice in our beds. They came in the dirty blankets we were issued. In the compound to the west of us are British Indian troops.

They are quite colorful with bright-colored turbans and black beards. They are also quite fierce-looking.

February 13   My wrists were chewed up by the bugs last night. Sprinkled my blankets and bed boards with delousing powder.

The life in Moosburg was hell. We could feel the bugs running over our bodies at night. Although some fellows got blood poisoning from the bites, the bugs seldom bothered me.

Despite the cold, damp weather, the Germans did not give us any fuel for heating the building, so we would stay in bed all day. The lighting was so poor that some of the fellows never did see what their beds looked like. Because of the crowded conditions, personal items were hung from the ceiling. I had a top bunk. I barely had room to lie down after hanging up my personal stuff. Sitting up was impossible.

The German food ration consisted of one half cup of warm water for breakfast, one cup of thin, watery soup for dinner, and a little black bread for supper with extra issues of cheese, margarine or blood sausage. For some time we had no Red Cross parcels and the fellows were really thin. We then received issues of parcels that had to last 2 weeks. At first we were issued British parcels which contained food that had to be cooked, but the

Germans would not give us any fuel. We made burners and blowers out of tin cans using the barbs from wire as nails. For fuel we first burned our bed boards and slung our sacks by nailing the burlap to the sides of the bed. When the bed boards gave out, we did a little more sabotage work and tore out the inner floor of the barracks. We also swiped sticks from the slot trenches. The Germans refused to clean out the outdoor latrines - one latrine for 2,000 men. It finally filled up and overflowed. As everyone was sick with the runs, you can imagine what a mess it created. It overflowed into the parade ground, so when the Germans told us to fall out for Appell to be counted, we refused to go. Finally, after several hours of tension, they promised to clean the latrine out, so we fell in.

Finally spring came and the renewed offensive of the Allies started pushing the Germans back. During the latter part of April, we saw fighter planes scouting our camp and on April 29th we were ordered inside the barracks as we could hear the big guns and machine guns. We could see American infantrymen advancing toward our camp and pushing toward the town of Moosburg. Then we heard the most welcome sound of all -- the rumble of American tanks.

When those tanks rolled into the prison compound, the Kriegies, P.O.W.'s -- unmindful of the live bullets still whistling through the air -- spilled out of the barracks and cheered the troops. After the shooting was over, a jeep with siren wailing and red light flashing came into the center of our compound. A soldier with a steel helmet, Eisenhower jacket, beautiful breaches and boots, and pearl-handled revolvers at his sides stood up on the hood of the jeep and gave us a pep talk which we didn't need. It was General Patton. I later learned that my first cousin, Dick Reardon, was a tank driver with the scouting tanks in front of Patton's main force.

May 7   After a week of liberation, we were still behind barbed wire. They were trucking us out as rapidly as they could, but it wasn't rapidly enough to suit us prisoners. Counting the various nationalities of prisoners, there were over 57,000 in this one camp. For example, on one side of us were Kerchas from India. On the other side of our compound were Russians.

The Russians were crazy. One night they were raising such a ruckus that the German guards told them that if they didn't quiet down that they would send several German dogs in to quiet them down. The next morning, the Russians threw the dog bones over the fence. The Russians had eaten the dogs!!

At the end of the first week of liberation, we were still behind barbed wire. Dutch and I found a pair of wire cutters and cut a hole in the fence. In search of an Army field kitchen, we started down a path through the woods when suddenly bullets were whistling by our heads. We ran like mad to a nearby river where we dove headfirst down the river bank. We crawled for a good half-mile on our hands and knees before we dared to stand up. We shortly thereafter located an army field kitchen where we found a sergeant and told him who we were and that we needed something to eat. He sat us down and brought to us two one-gallon jars of strawberry jam and fresh white bread.

We almost killed ourselves wolfing down this food. Then he arranged for a truck to take us back to camp. That was the last time we left camp until we were trucked out to LaHavre.

And so ended my miraculous war journey. I firmly believe that it was the will of God that kept me alive during those dangerous times. I also believe that my eternal optimism and positive attitude toward life served me well in very difficult situations. After the war, I held no ill feelings toward my enemies and even went to work for the American branch of a German firm.

Returning Home

I entered RIT in the fall of 1945 and interviewed with Dr. Ralph L. VanPersem. He allowed me to enter the Chemistry Department if I would enter night school the first year to enroll in basic chemistry and math as well as taking the regular first year program. This I accomplished with great success but it took a great deal of effort.

During the second week in December 1945, I was standing in the main corridor at R.I.T. with several classmates when one of them asked me who I was taking to the Christmas dance. I said, "Are you crazy? You know I don't have a girlfriend and I don't want a girlfriend until I get out of college." One of my friends said, "We are all going to the Christmas dance and we want you to get a date." To which I replied, "I'm not going so stop bothering me!"

The next day we were standing in the same spot when one of the fellows said to me, "In a few minutes a great looking girl is going to come around the corner. Take a look at her and tell us what you think." When the girl came into view, my mouth fell open and I said, "I'm going to marry that girl!" Her name was Eddella Griswold and I took her to the Christmas dance. On August 3, 1946 we were married and we will be celebrating 61 years of marriage this coming August 3, 2007.

Upon graduating from the Chemistry Department at RIT, I went to work as a laboratory technician at Distillation Products.

I was given charge of the company's Helium Leak Detector Program and succeeded so well that I soon became the company's trouble shooter and installation Engineer. I was soon put in charge of the company's thin film laboratory under Dr. Bancroft.

When our West Coast Sales Engineer, Carl Hermann, resigned to go into business for himself, he recommended me as his replacement. As a result, my wife Eddella and I, sold our property in Rochester and along with our children, Patricia, Suzanne and Robby, moved to Los Altos, California where I became the West Coast Sales Manager with the eleven western states along with Alaska and Hawaii.

I was very successful in this position with a rapid growth in the western market. I established branch offices in Los Angeles and Seattle. In a couple more years, the Distillation Products Division was merged into the parent company Consolidated Electronics Corporation of Pasadena and we were named the Consolidated Vacuum Division in Rochester, New York.

After considerable effort, I convinced Consolidated Vacuum that the west coast market would grow considerably faster if we would establish a systems fabrication operation in Palo Alto, California with its own manager. This new operation became a huge success.

Upon learning of Lockheed's plans to sale source the purchase of a large space chamber for the testing of space vehicles at their Mountain View, California plant, I immediately contacted our headquarters office located in Rochester, New York, about this pending contract to a competitive company.

I contacted the Engineering Department at Lockheed and discussed with them that I had learned that they were purchasing a space chamber being designed exclusively for them and asked if my company, Consolidated Vacuum, could submit a competitive bid for the project which Lockheed agreed to.

We were one week away from submitting our bid and I asked Ed Perkins when he was going to write our proposal. He said, "I just don't have the time. You're going to have to write it." I went into a state of shock but wound up writing a proposal which I could be proud of and we were awarded the contract.

Within the next year, Consolidated Vacuum Corporation was awarded the contract for the space simulator chamber installed at NASA Air Jet Propulsion Laboratory in Pasadena, California. I'm proud to say that within the next year, I was transferred back to our headquarters in Rochester, New York, and promoted to Vice President of Marketing.

In 1963, I moved my family to Monroeville, Pennsylvania where I accepted the position of Executive Vice-President and President of Leybold-Heraeus, Inc.

In 1967, I was elected President of the Norwalk Company, a subsidiary of the Union Corporation of Verona, Pennsylvania. After one year, I was promoted to the position of Group Vice-President with five companies reporting to me including the Norwalk Company. The other companies assigned to me are as follows.

Bob and Children: Patricia, Suzanne and Robby

The Johnson Family — Suzanne, Bob, Patricia, Eddella and Robby

Bob and Eddella Johnson

Union Corporation
Group Vice-President
Robert O. Johnson

Norwalk Company

Manufacturers of a complete line of air and gas compressors. World wide distribution with sales representatives in many countries.

Norwalk Turbo

Compressors powered by aircraft engines.

Kol-Flo, Inc.

Manufacturers of carbonation and water purification system for the soft drink industry.

Flonetics Corp.

Designer and manufacturer of complicated requirements for valves.

Autotronic Products, Inc.

Specialized in printed circuit boards.

I retired in 1986.

Military Background During World War II

U.S. Army Air Force: October 1942 to October 1945

First Lieutenant, Pilot
B24 Bomber

- Forty-five Missions over European Theatre
- Shot down over what is now Western Poland on July 7, 1944
- Prisoner of War of the Germans for 10 months in Stalag Luft III Sagan and Stam Lager VII A Prisoner of War Camps
- Liberated by General Patton on April 29, 1945

Holder of: Purple Heart
               Air Medal with 4 Oak-Leaf Clusters

Robert O. Johnson, President, The Norwalk Company, 1982

Resume

Business Experience

All of my business experience has been in the high vacuum field. As of September of this year, I will have been associated with Consolidated Vacuum Corporation and its various predecessor organizations for a period of 18 years. Following is a summary of my experience during that time.

September 1945 – June 1948

Worked at Distillation Products Industries while attending the Rochester Institute of Technology. During this period, I spent my time at first as an inspector in the Quality Control Department and later in the Development Laboratory under Mr. Ben Dayton assisting in the design and testing of diffusion pumps, valves, and baffles.

1949 - 1950

Worked under Dr. George Bancroft as a laboratory technician in charge of the company's Helium Mass Spectrometer Leak Detector Program involving complete responsibility for the application and maintenance of a new and, at the time, a very complicated and troublesome piece of vacuum instrumentation. My successful handling of this assignment, I firmly believe, contributed immeasurably in gaining the confidence of DPI's management and lead to the many challenging opportunities which were given me in the years to follow.

1951 – October 1953
        Supervisor of Vacuum Deposition Development
Laboratory under Dr. Bancroft. In this capacity, I directed
two laboratory technicians in the development of new
applications, both functional and decorative, for vacuum
deposition equipment. During this period, I also did
extensive traveling for the company installing and servicing
vacuum deposition equipment and also did consulting work
on the process. In connection with this work in 1953, I
authored an article published in Precision Casting
Magazine entitled, "No Polishing Needed", which dealt
with the method and economics of vacuum metallizing of
zinc die castings.

October 1953 – April 1955
        Held position of Western Field Sales Manager with
headquarters in Palo Alto, California. I was responsible for
sales and service of CVC's complete line of vacuum
products in the eleven western states plus Western Canada,
Alaska, and Hawaii. This assignment was handled entirely
by me and one secretary.

April 1955 – July 1959
        In April of 1955, CVC's marketing department was
merged into CEC's Central Marketing Organization. At
this time, I was promoted to the position of District Sales
Manager of the San Francisco District with responsibility
for the sales and service of all of CEC's products including
mass spectrometers, leak detectors, recording ascillographs,
pressure transducers, magnetic tape recorders, date
acquisition and processing systems as well as vacuum
products.

During this period I hired, trained and supervised a staff of 14 people including five Sales Engineers, three Service Engineers and three Secretaries. In addition, I had three people working in connection with the warehousing and distribution of vacuum products. I was also instrumental in establishing and organizing CVC's West Coast Distribution Center during this period. Today this is a major operation and has contributed materially to the growth of CVC's business in the western states.

This assignment gave me the opportunity of becoming well versed in many phases of sales management, warehousing, distribution, order service, sales quotas, territorial assignment, budgeting, expense control, sales forecasting, and recruiting, soliciting and training personnel.

July 1959 – July 1962

In July 1959, CVC was incorporated as a wholly owned subsidiary of CEC and was given authorization to establish its own marketing department independent of CEC's Central Marketing organization.

My prime interest being in the high vacuum field, I transferred from Central Marketing to CVC and shortly thereafter I was appointed Western Regional Sales Manager. Initially, my staff consisted of two Secretaries and two Warehouse men in Palo Alto and one Sales Engineer and a Secretary in Los Angeles to cover the western half of the United States. Within the next three years as business grew, I established offices in Seattle, Washington, Albuquerque, New Mexico, and Dallas, Texas. I also expanded both the Palo Alto and Los Angeles offices.

During this three year period, we quadrupled our business in the Western Region. By July 1962, the Western Region had a total complement of nineteen people including myself. I was also assisted in the organization of a West Coast Assembly Plant for CVC in Palo Alto, California. Although this operation did not report to me, I worked very closely with the Plant Manager in setting it up.

July 1962 – October 1962
   In July of 1962, I was transferred back to Rochester, New York and promoted to the office of Vice-President of Field Sales.

October 1962 – December 1963
   In October 1962, I was promoted to the office of Vice-President of Marketing. In this position, I have full responsibility for CVC's entire marketing operation including field sales, advertising, sales promotion, public relations, application engineering, order service and export. I have under me, seventy people in the Marketing Department and responsibility for an annual operating budget well in excess of one million dollars.

December 1963 – February 1970
   I took the position of Executive Vice-President and President of Leybold-Heraeus, Inc. in Monroeville, Pennsylvania.

February 1970 – 1986 (Retired)
   I took the position of President of the Norwalk Company, Inc. in Norwalk Connecticut. In 1972, I was appointed Group Vice-President of The Union Corporation, the Norwalk Company's parent corporation. My area of

responsibility on the corporate level encompassed the Norwalk Company as well as four other subsidiaries of The Union Corporation. During this time I became a Trustee of the Connecticut Public Expenditure Council and a member of City Trust's Advisory Board for the Norwalk Region and was a Director of Norwalk's Chamber of Commerce. I also accepted Mayor William A. Collins' invitation to be a member of his Task Force to assist the City of Norwalk in evaluating the feasibility of a DHC system through a community consensus. I also served on the Task Force of the Norwalk Redevelopment Agency and the Norwalk Planning and Zoning Office's Advisory Committee for the protection of the surrounding waterways. In addition, I was also an Honorary Member of the Arts Council of the City of Norwalk. I retired in 1986.

Education
        1945-1948, Rochester Institute of Technology – graduated with a certificate in Chemistry.
        1948-1953, University of Rochester – attended evenings talking additional courses in physical sciences and liberal arts.

Military
        Spent three years (1942-1945) in the United States Army Air Force. Honorably discharged with the rank of 1st Lt. and rating of Four Engine Aircraft Commander.

<u>Organizations</u>
American Management Association
American Vacuum Society
American Society for Metals

The Beast

On a beautiful, bright July day at high noon, an American plane on its longest bombing mission over Poland, was hit and caught fire. The plane crashed to earth taking the tail gunner with it. The pilots and crew parachuted to earth. The plane was fresh off the assembly line in the states and had not been given a name. It crashed outside a village in the southern part of Poland.

As years went by, the story of the American plane was hushed by villagers, but two little boys interested in World War II, heard the story and were fascinated by it. They had dreamed of being pilots too and continued their search of the plane as they grew into manhood.

In 2003, they found the plane with Geiger counters. It was buried under sixty years of dirt and debris, but little by little they uncovered over 150 pieces of the plane and thus started the saga of "The Beast", the name they gave the plane.

Greetings!

Dear Mr Johnson at the beginning I would like to introduce myself. I'm 38 years old. I live in Poland in small village Krupski Młyn. I and my friends are interested in history of II World War. We admire courage, bravery, heroism and devotion of pilots who took part in that war. To sit down behind the B-24 rudders is something what we are dreaming about.

We know that you flight in II World War over the area of Poland and your plane was shot down in the mission to Odertal at 7th July 1944. The place of catastrophe of your B-24 ("Beast") is near Krupski Młyn. For 60 years history of your crashed plane was a secret. Now we want to find out what really happened. We are also going to make a movie which will show the tragical flight of your B-24. We visited the place of catastrophe and with help of metal detector we found many parts of "Beast" (for example: AERIAL DEAD RECONING COMPUTER TYPE E-6B kept in good condition in leather case). To make a movie we need many information and documents if they saved. We would also like to meet members of the airplane.

We decide to write a few sentences to you and ask you a few questions about catastrophe. We would be very grateful if you will answer. We promise that when we will finish our movie we send you a copy (with English translation).

Here are our questions:

1. In which part of airplane the bullets hit and what problems in navigability of airplane this caused?
2. Who became wounded in airplane?
3. What was the emergency plan in case of shoot down?
4. You jumped out from the plane at 11.30 about one kilometre on the North East from Schwieben City (polish name: Świbie). Did you return to the place where the plane fell down?
5. What did you do with your personal weapon, papers, maps and equipment? If it is hidden could you tell us where?
6. Who arrested you? What time was it? Where did it happen?
7. Where were you taken on examination? Who examined you?
8. Did everybody from airplane's members who survived the catastrophe was taken to the Dulag Luft Oberusel camp?
9. From which city were you taken to the camp?
10. Were the life conditions in the camp good?
11. How did you regain freedom?
12. What did you do after II World War?
13. What do you do now?

I send you pictures of parts of airplane and pictures of Krupski Młyn. If you would like to contact me these are our adresses:

1) Andrzej Jaworski
   ul. Prusa 15/7
   42 - 693 Krupski Młyn
   POLAND

2) Jacek Kiszkis
   e-mail: jkiszkis@nitron.com.pl

I wish you much health!
Sincerely yours

Andrzej Jaworski

P.S. Sorry for my English

INFORMATION
ON PLANNIG OF A DOCUMENTARY FILM

It happened on the seventh day of August 1944, around 1130 hrs. The 15th American Air Army, operating out of southern Italy bombarded the (German, TM) IG Farben works in Sud Blechhammer manufacturing gasoline from coal. Because of the strategic importance of the plant the US bombers appeared there rather frequently. Their the task was destroying the fuel industry of the III Reich. The plant was one of the best protected objects which made the assignment difficult and in the course of this raid one of the American B-24 was hit by German AA fire

The plane managed to reach Krupski Mlyn (Polish name given to the then German locality, TM) where it crashed, about 2 km north of the center of the town. Several members of the crew managed to survive, as witnessed by Eleonora Berger and Joahim Haus living there then but now residing outside Poland (TM). The reports of the witnesses were verified by the discovery by two present residents of Krupski Mlyn of a substantial number of equipment elements, parts of the steering and navigation equipment. The search area agrees with the data found in the German archives. Our objective is to preserve those interesting events for posterity by presenting them in film. The project would show a small part of general history and enrich local history by facts likely to be forgotten. The film would not only be a reconstruction of the fateful moments for the crew but, above all, it would illustrate the search for truth about that event.

We are in possession of a large quantity of archival material, among it documents of the American Army showing the time before and after the crash. We also have Xerox copies of German documents related to the fate of the crew. We habe been in contact with Robert Johnson and George E. Shehanen, former members of the crew, and with Joseph F. Chalkerein, historian of the 454 Bombardiment Group Association, Inc., who are interested in our project and declared their readiness in helping with pictures and detailed description of the flight and the crash.

We have established contact with the commanding officer in Lubliniec (Poland), who agreed to allow us to film in restricted military areas and to film parachute jumps there. We have also contacted the US Consulate in Krakow with the intention of inviting it to accept the patronage over the venture. We have met with an enthusiastic reception for our project from the past and current inhabitants of Krupski Mlyn.

We wish to stress that this is a non-profit project. We estimate the cost of the venture at about 35,000 zloty.* Our own input would be preparatory work, compiling historical material, producing of the script and realization of the final product. In this connection we are seeking sponsors who would support us financially (purchases of material, leasing of special equipment, covering actors' fees etc). Sponsoring firms and institutions will be allowed short commercial messages. The subject of the film would be the tragic fate of an American bomber and its crew.

*ca $10,480 (US)

Dear Andrzej and Jacek,

I am forwarding a copy of a photograph taken in my office and behind me can be seen a large collection of military airplanes. I was a Group Vice-President of five companies including Norwalk Turbo and it was managed by Dr. Karl Pilorczak. Dr. Pilorczak was a native Pole who was captured and forced into a labor camp in a stone quarry by the Germans. His wife, a native Pole, was forced into slave labor also. They later met, married and migrated to London where Dr. Pilorczak obtained his doctor's degree in engineering. He was a brilliant engineer and designed for the Norwalk Turbo Company, a line of gas compressors which were powered by aircraft engines. Incidentally, Dr. Pilorczak and his wife still carry on their arms a tattoo identifying them as Polish prisoners of war by the Germans.

On another subject, I want to mention that I am writing a book on my military experience as well as my industrial experience after the war which I would be willing to share with you on a non-exclusive basis. The title of my book is "I'm Coming Home." When I left for the war to join my combat unit in Italy, I told my mother that if she were ever to receive word that I was shot down in combat, that she should always remember that "I'm coming home." My book will include my family tree, military history including my flight training, and highlights of my combat experience before being shot down. I also cover my imprisonment in Stalag Luft III in Poland and details of the Death March precipitated by oncoming Russian forces and my subsequent imprisonment in Mooseberg. After my liberation by General Patton, I returned to the United States and pursued a college education and a career in industrial sales.

Please let me know how much of this information you might be interested in for your project. I look forward to hearing from you in the near future.

Sincerely,

Robert O. Johnson

I, Robert Orson Johnson, was born at 11:55 A.M. on March 20, 1922. At birth I weighed 9 pounds and measured 20 inches. I was born at my Aunt Mary's home in Fairport, New York. My middle name of Orson comes from my grandfather, Orson Johnson, who, unfortunately, was killed by a New York Central freight train.

My father, Leslie S. Johnson, was descended from relatives migrating from England on the ship that followed the *Mayflower* and eventually settled in upstate New York. He was a member of the Hicks family, which migrated to the New World on the 11th day of November 1621, the ship *Fortune* arrived at Plymouth, Massachusetts from London. She followed the *Mayflower* bringing over parts of families left behind by those who came in that famous vessel the year before.

In the Fortune, with this second body of Puritans cane Robert Hicks, the ancestor of the family in America. He was a leather-dresser from Bermondesey Street, Southwark, London. His father, James Hicks, was lineally descended from Ellis Hicks who was knighted by Edward, the Black Prince, on the battlefield of Poictiers September 9, 1346 for bravery in capturing a set of colors from the French.

Margaret, the wife of Robert Hicks, and her children came over on the ship *Ann*, which arrived at Plymouth during the latter part of June 1622. This family settled in Duxbury, Massachusetts, but two of the sons, John and Stephen, subsequently came to Long Island.

In October 1645, Governor Kieft granted a patent to Thomas Farrington, John Hicks, and others for the township of Flushing, Long Island. John Hicks seems to have taken a leading part in the affairs of the settlement and was appointed at various times to fill the most important offices. His name and that of his son Thomas appears in connection with almost every public measure for many years.

Robert O. Johnson died January 21, 2008 in New Bern, North Carolina at the age of 85.